'I started my fitness regimen at Leena Mogre's fitness centre in Thane. I could see the discipline and professionalism of the trainers along with world-class equipment there. But it was only when I became additional commissioner of police for Mumbai city that I had an occasion to get acquainted with the truly inspiring legend of the fitness industry—Leena Mogre. She organized a workshop on fitness for the IPS Officers' Wives Association. She is full of incessant energy, bubbling enthusiasm and tremendous willpower. She always supports programmes we organize for cops' fitness and diet awareness. She has earned a reputation and name of her own in this male-dominated industry'—Vishwas Nagre Patil, IPS officer

'Leena introduced me to power yoga and it has now become the mantra of my life. Every body is unique and reacts differently to different forms of fitness. Leena understands that and finds your best fit'—Sameera Reddy, actress

'I have been working out with Leena Mogre for the past five years. Her tremendous growth speaks for itself. From being India's first woman personal trainer to starting her own signature brand of fitness centres in India, she is great at what she does and yet down to earth. Leena and her better half, Nikhil, make a great team together. She has an amazing clientele. Everyone from movies to the corporate world to the fashion industry come to her to get their bodies in shape' —Candice Pinto, model

'Leena is a veteran expert who has a passion and commitment to her work. Her keen interest in each of her clients and the ambition to excel in her work has made her a force to be reckoned with in her field'—Neeta Lulla, designer

'Leena Mogre is best known as the face of fitness. But I have known her as my sister-in-law. She has made the whole family proud with her determination to change people's looks and lives. The only words to describe her are devoted, dedicated, passionate and strong. These apply to Leena not just as a fitness expert but also as a mum and a wife'—Shilpa Shirodkar, actress

'Leena defines fitness in her own unique and youthful way. Revolutionizing the fitness industry, she has covered all facets of working out, right from functional training to kick-boxing, yoga to weight training. With her array of nutrition facts and diets, one is sure to be on his or her way to a healthier life'—Madhur Bhandarkar, film-maker

'Leena Mogre's passion for fitness is contagious. To avoid catching it and developing a chronically healthy lifestyle, do not read this book!'—Rahul Khanna, actor

'I know everyone in the fitness business. Or so I thought a decade ago. All the gym owners, the world-champion bodybuilders, I knew them all. Then one day this unknown girl walked into my office with a great air of confidence and said, "I am having a press conference on fitness, and you are the chief guest." At no point did she say "would you consider" or "would you accept". That was my first meeting with Leena Mogre. I asked her if she owned a gym, or dealt in fitness products. What did she do in the world of beefy men who are mostly seen as body parts and rarely as complete people (Bicep dekh, check out that calf, etc.)? She said that she trained trainers. Wow, I thought, that was different and went for the press conference. I wasn't given a chance to refuse anyway. I knew this girl would go far. And she has. Much more than I had imagined.

'We have since kept in touch. I went for her training academy's certificate distribution ceremony, then for meetings when she was setting up an international gym chain here, and then when she was setting up her own chain of gyms. All the time I was thinking, "Bodybuilding is truly a man's world. How the hell does this girl beat all the men at their own game and rise to the top?" But she has.

'And just when I think that she has done it all, she goes and writes a book. I am sure it's going to be a bestseller, if her track record is something to go by'—Bharat Dabholkar, ad man

'When Leena approached me to start an academy to help people become trainers twenty-six years ago, it was a revolution in Mumbai and, in fact, India. With her determination, dedication and discipline, she has taken it to new heights. In twenty-six years, this is one woman who hasn't put on weight and looks like the same fit person she was. It's been a pleasure to read the real success story of Leena'
—Dr Vithal Venkatesh Kamat

'Leena is so self-motivated. She has immense energy which helps people like me train better. Her gyms are equipped for sports-specific training and that makes my work easier. If Leena is standing by your side, your health and your entire lifestyle is in safe hands'—Yuvraj Singh, cricketer

'I have known Leena for a long time. Whenever I felt like giving up, she has always told me to ask myself, "Why have I started it all?" It reminds me of all the hard work I have put in so far on my fitness and motivates me to never give up'—Rohit (Timmy) Narang

'Leena Mogre is probably the first person in Mumbai to put diet, fitness and gym workouts on the map. Over the years, she and her team have trained countless models of mine and taught them fitness for life. She should have written her book twenty years ago!'—Maureen Wadia, president, Gladrags Beauty Pageants, and editor, *Gladrags*

'Leena Mogre is a fitness expert of repute. I have personally seen her commitment and dedication to the cause of personal fitness and lifestyle management. She is disciplined and experienced and we wish her every success in the publication of her book, *Total Fitness*. Can't wait to buy my copy'—Vivek B. Singh, joint managing director, Procam International

TOTAL FITNESS

11th Sept. 2018

Dearest Rupa, & Pradip,

Be Fit!

Be Happy!

A beginners guide to fitness.

Leenalloque

Dearest Aunsha &
Uncle,

Be Fit!
Be Happy!

A beginners guide to
fitness. Jenny

Jenn Mayne

TOTAL FITNESS

THE
LEENA MOGRE
WAY

RANDOM HOUSE INDIA

Published by Random House India in 2015
1

Copyright © Leena Mogre 2015
Foreword copyright © Madhuri Dixit 2015

Random House Publishers India Pvt Ltd
7th Floor, Infinity Tower C, DLF Cyber City
Gurgaon – 122002
Haryana

Random House Group Limited
20 Vauxhall Bridge Road
London SW1V 2SA
United Kingdom

978 81 8400 436 6

This book is sold subject to the condition that it shall not, by way of trade or otherwise, be lent, resold, hired out, or otherwise circulated without the publisher's prior consent in any form of binding or cover other than that in which it is published and without a similar condition including this condition being imposed on the subsequent purchaser.

Typeset in Sabon by R. Ajith Kumar

Printed and bound in India by Replika Press Private Limited

A PENGUIN RANDOM HOUSE COMPANY

*To my mother, Mrs Sanjeevani Pendse, and
my late mother-in-law, Mrs Nalini Mogre,
who were my pillars of strength.*

*And to my late father-in-law, Mr Keshav Mogre,
who has been my biggest inspiration in fitness.*

Contents

Foreword by Madhuri Dixit   xiii
Introduction   xvii

Chapter 1: Your True Potential   1
Chapter 2: Myths about Fitness   23
Chapter 3: Starting Out   39
Chapter 4: Working Out at Your Fitness Level   53
Chapter 5: Sustaining Your Workout   67
Chapter 6: Fad Diets   83
Chapter 7: Managing Your Lifestyle   99
Chapter 8: Popular Problems   117
Conclusion: The Leena Mogre Way   149

A Note on the Author   155
Acknowledgements   159

Foreword

WHEN I THINK OF LEENA, I automatically think of fitness. She has been working in the health industry for more than two decades and has been at the forefront of the fitness revolution in Bollywood. She understood the importance of fitness when few else in India did, and has trained not only actors but also trainers so that they can help more people to stay fit.

I have known Leena since my *Hum Aapke Hain Kaun* days. She was my first trainer and has helped me understand my body and how important it is to look slim and feel healthy. During those days we didn't have any iPods and I used to carry my 2-in-1 and dumb-bells around on the sets much to the amusement of my colleagues and fellow actors. How things have changed now! Most actors I know today have a strict exercise regimen and take really good care of their bodies.

I have always believed that a healthy and fit body is the essence of true happiness and success in life. No matter what profession you are in, if you feel good, it reflects in your personality. And, to me, this is what Leena stands for, a wealth of experience and knowledge who can change your life and give you Total Fitness.

I think this book is a must for everybody and there is something all of us can learn from it. I wish her all the best and hope you enjoy reading *Total Fitness*.

Madhuri Dixit
Mumbai, 2015

Introduction

I KNOW WHAT IT FEELS like. The alarm on your phone ringing by your ear, and the realization that you have to get out of your warm, snug bed and go to the gym. It will mean your body hurting for an hour and you feeling jealous of your disciplined friends.

But if you've worked out even once in your life, you know how amazing your body and mind feel when you leave the gym. You feel energized, ready to take on any challenge, and the hot body is a lovely bonus. They say that the greatest distance is between your bed and your shoes. Once you cover that distance the rest is easy.

That's how I started on this road to where I am. I have been fit and active all my life. But that didn't prevent me from gaining 31 kg during my first

Introduction

pregnancy. No one thought I'd be able to lose that weight. They said I'd be like those women who give up or lose interest once they have a child. Of course, I had to prove them wrong. It took me a year, a long time considering my masters degree in food science and nutrition, but I did come down to my original weight of 53 kg.

While this achievement did give me the push to enter the fitness industry wholeheartedly, I had been dabbling in it for a while. It was in 1994–95 that hotelier Vithal Kamat, who was also a family friend, told me to start an aerobics class at his club in Vile Parle, a suburb of Mumbai. At that time, there were very few people certified to teach aerobics and I wanted to be one of them. I formulated a basic course outline and then, along with a few medical professionals, worked on the entire course certification and the manual. I was one of the ten women who joined the class; I was one of the first students of my own course. Shortly afterwards, I started personal training and became the first woman personal trainer in India. My first celebrity client was Madhuri Dixit. She was such a sweet woman. Soon I got an offer to be the CEO of an international chain

Introduction

of gyms. I was there for four years. But I wanted to start something of my own. And that's how Leena Mogre's Fitness came about. I've started six gyms—four in Mumbai and one each in Nashik and Chandigarh—in eight years. Going on from there, I am proud to say that actors like Ranbir Kapoor, Kareena Kapoor, Bipasha Basu, Deepika Padukone, Jacqueline Fernandez and Katrina Kaif started their first workouts with me.

WHAT FITNESS MEANS TO ME

For most of my life, I have enjoyed being active and I identify as an exercise enthusiast. While my reasons for exercising and being active have changed over time, I can't really think of a time in my life when I didn't value physical activity. Like most people, when I was younger I didn't think a lot about the long-term health benefits. I enjoyed being active. With age has come the wisdom that there is much more to exercise and physical activity than looking a certain way. For me, fitness has a lot to do with how I feel and how functional my body is. My son's friend recently came to our house during the Ganapati celebrations. He touched everyone's feet, but said he felt weird touching my feet because I look just a little older than my 24-year-old son Arjun. It was so wonderful to hear that. It just means that all the effort I put into looking fit is showing. To me, being fit is all about feeling strong, capable, and making myself less vulnerable to injury, illness and disease. I exercise because I want my body to feel like it is working *for* me rather than *against* me. I want to feel strong and capable of carrying out the tasks of everyday life, and, of course, there is the added benefit of looking young.

I believe that fitness is a lifestyle. It's like brushing your teeth. You do that every day, don't you? So why can't you work towards making yourself fit every day? A lot of people ask me what will happen if they stop working out. And I always ask them, 'What will happen if you stop brushing your teeth every day?' Your teeth will rot and fall. You have to integrate fitness into your life, just the way you make time for your meals.

Fitness is preventive medicine. A lot of your problems are solved by taking preventive action. 90 per cent of the people who start working out do it so that they can lose weight. Very few people go to the gym to become fit.

Fitness, for me, is also strength of mind, body and spirit. The obvious benefits are the physical gains of strength, flexibility and endurance. However, there are numerous less obvious benefits too. The feeling of strength and self-confidence that comes from being physically active may not be the reason why someone begins a fitness programme, but is very often why people stay with it. Being physically active changes how we think, reduces stress and increases positive outlooks. It helps us handle any problem that crops up because we have the mental strength to deal with it. Working out is meditation for me.

Fitness is really about maximizing one's potential. It's more than just exercising. It's about finding the willpower to show up for your workouts without fail. It's about finding a reason to get that workout done when you are warm and cosy in bed and all you want to do is hit that Snooze button. Fitness is focusing on what you can control, not what you can't.

Being fit and healthy means eating well, being well rested, and feeling strong and happy. Some things are beyond your own control, like genetics, but other

Introduction

things are within your control. This is where you can try to manage your life to feel healthy. I try to eat a balanced diet every day and minimize sugars and carbs. Trying to be healthy means fitting exercise into your life on a regular basis and doing something you really enjoy.

I give a lot of talks at corporate and other events. While what I say differs depending on what they want me to talk about, there's one thing I always include: we spend so much of our time and effort in planning our careers and finances, but why don't we actively plan our physical fitness as well? If you don't plan your fitness, all your money planning will go haywire. You may not be healthy enough to spend all that money you've earned. All that hard-earned money will go to the hospital's ICU.

Being fit is like being in love with yourself. Unless you worship and respect your body, nobody else will. Whatever stress you have, being fit will ensure that you wake up with a smile. That makes facing the stress easier. Stress is inevitable in life. Being fit will help you get through your day without an aching body and a tired mind.

Introduction

How my brand of fitness is different

At Leena Mogre's Fitness, we give a lot of personal attention to our clients. Every gym proclaims to do that, but we actually practise it. Every person who enrols with us goes through a very in-depth, one-hour fitness assessment that's not just about standing on a machine and taking notes on your weight and measurements. We do a complete check-up, at the end of which we have a graph. Based on it, we decide on a workout schedule. Even the calorie intake is planned accordingly. This assessment has even helped us ward off emergencies. Once, a young boy was on the cardiorespiratory test when he became very breathless on the treadmill. His parents, both doctors, immediately rushed him to the hospital where they found that he had a heart problem that had gone undetected for so long. If we had directly started his workouts without assessing him, he would have died on the treadmill. We also conduct a psychological analysis. If a member is aggressive, we prescribe exercises accordingly.

I do not see this as a mere profession. It is my passion. It makes me happy to see the transformation in people. We have a variety of exercises to keep our members interested and ensure that monotony doesn't creep in. We also include diet in our prescription. There have been people who have lost more than 50 kg. We ensure that they lose weight the right way. Our timings are also very helpful. Our gym in Bandra, Mumbai, is open 24/7. Another gym in Mumbai is open from 5 a.m. to 11 p.m. And, of course, we update our trainers regularly. The atmosphere in our gym is very different from what you find in other gyms. We treat all our members equally because everyone pays the same money. A celebrity is treated the same way as any other member. Everyone follows the same rules.

How this book will help you

With all the information freely available on the Internet, it is hard for even the most experienced fitness enthusiasts to navigate through the facts and myths. It can be difficult to discern the difference between what really works and what is just too good to be true. In addition, there are so many fitness goals and so many different ways to achieve

Introduction

them that you simply do not know what to follow.

This book will clear up all the misconceptions people have about fitness. As the fitness industry has evolved, so have the misconceptions and perceptions. There are so many things you need to keep in mind when you are working out. A lot of people say that gymming is not essential, just yoga or running is enough. But weight training is the foundation of your fitness regimen. That, however, doesn't mean yoga deserves a less important place. Similarly, a lot of odd diets have also stemmed up from nowhere. One needs to be wise in fitness planning.

This book has everything that I have learned in my twenty years in this industry. What I really want this book to accomplish is for everyone to start loving fitness. Most people work out because they have to. I want people to do it because they *want* to. Being fit can change your life in so many wonderful ways. And this book will show you how.

POINTS TO PONDER

- You brush your teeth every day, don't you? So why can't you work out daily?

- Fitness is about waking up in the morning and going to bed at night with a peaceful mind and a smile on your face, and not complaining about an aching body and a tired mind.

- Fitness is focusing on what you can control, not what you can't.

Chapter 1

Your True Potential

THE GOAL OF MOST PEOPLE, if I assume correctly, is to live their best life—a life that is fulfilling, joyful and better than what they hoped for. Personally, I believe this is possible only with a body that helps me live my best life. And the only way to achieve this is to eat and be fit. You may wonder why I am advocating eating what you want. But what's a good life without the joy of food? That is why I never recommend that anyone deny themselves the happiness that food brings. And talking about joy, why should you have to wear clothes you don't like? Because you want to hide your body? Everyone should be able to wear clothes they like that flatter their body. It is possible to do the things you want to do, eat what you want and wear the clothes that you love. The answer is fitness—eating and then working out.

It is not only about looking good; it is about feeling fit internally. That is a philosophy every gym and fitness professional has. But my philosophy is that you have to plan for your fitness. I want you to visualize what your life will be five years from now. Life is only going to get tougher and more difficult. Many people visit my gym and enrol only after a month, or sometimes more. It takes them that long to take out time for themselves. Your gym appointment should be like your parlour appointment. Do you miss the appointment to get waxed or your eyebrows shaped? So why miss the important date you have with your body?

Some people take great pride in their sicknesses. They talk about how they suffer from so much stress and blood pressure and then pat themselves on the back for managing life despite these problems. They expect everyone to admire them for doing everyday tasks. But you could do so much more—and do it better—if you were fitter. If you are fit, you enjoy your life a lot more. Fitness is the base for everything.

You can have good hair, good skin, good posture, positive attitude and you're always on a high. Weight loss and being in shape is only one of the many benefits of fitness. If you are fit, your lean muscle tissue is always good. So you don't put on weight and your basal metabolic rate (BMR) is always high. Fitness brings great discipline into your life. You learn to say no to bad food and people. So many people encourage you to forget about your diet for a day when you are out with them. And when you say no, people respect you for that.

Buy a pair of jeans that is one size smaller and hang it on the right side of your cupboard. So every time you open it, that's the first thing you see. Let that pair of jeans motivate you to get the body you have always wanted. One day you will be able to pull it above your hips after months of being stuck there. The joy of finally fitting into it will be unmatched.

If you feel good about the way you look, you will automatically be in a good frame of mind and hence ultimately have good health. And that's how you will be able to handle the stresses of life. I have gone through a lot of ups and downs while setting up my business. In the past two or three years, I have dealt with a lot of problems. I have faced sabotage issues for a while now. All this created a lot of chaos in my life. But I have fought all of them. And a lot of credit goes to the fact that I am fit—mentally and physically. It has helped me face life better. And it has enabled me to see positivity in any problem.

Fitness also automatically ensures against diseases because you are eating right. You have a disciplined lifestyle. And, of course, everyone goes through emotional ups and downs in life. But even when you are depressed, you pull yourself to the gym. I concede that it is not easy. But I have seen people who are feeling low or sad push themselves in the gym and go back home happier. They have sweated the day's stress out, and the next day is another day.

What Total Fitness means

There's a bodybuilder called Rachel McLish who once said, 'Never be satisfied with looking good, when you can look absolutely lethal.' This is true for both men and women. A lot of people say that you should accept your age with grace. That does not mean that you become overweight and let yourself go. Working out even when you are older does not mean you are fighting the effects of age. You are just getting in shape and being healthy. I have noticed that women usually let themselves go after the age of 30. They get married by then and have children, and think they should devote more time to that life than on themselves. But how can you take care of your family members when you are struggling with your own health and fitness?

Most women are thin and fit when they are in college and are happy with their bodies. Then comes work life, where a desk job results in gradual weight gain. Soon, the woman is married and has gained 5 kg. The kids bring more weight gain and when she looks in the mirror ten years down the line, she does not recognize herself. That's where the starvation and obsession with diets begin because no one wants to lose weight the healthy way, for the healthy way requires effort and hard work. At the end of this, the woman's BMR and body system is screwed up. So many years of abuse, and when she finally comes to the gym, she wants instant results!

That's where our fitness assessment at Leena Mogre's Fitness comes in. It is like a blood report that helps the doctor diagnose the problem. It is a one-hour test where we check a person's body fat percentage, measurements, cardiorespiratory capacity, muscle strength, muscle endurance, flexibility, grip strength and abdominal strength. At the end of it, we have a graph that shows us the person's body capacity. Then, looking at the results, we plan the person's whole fitness schedule along with a lifestyle management programme. We don't call our programmes weight-loss programmes because we concentrate on reducing the fat percentage that is inside the body. In our lifestyle management programme, we first focus on detoxifying, then managing the carbohydrate–protein ratio, and then move on to teaching clients how to maintain that balance for life. Here we teach you how to manage your life even when you stop coming to the gym. That is because you cannot possibly be on a diet throughout your life. But you can exercise throughout your life. Lifestyle management is important because you will be travelling, partying, eating out, living your life.

How to know how fit you are

When you know your fitness level, you can set realistic fitness goals, monitor your progress and stay motivated. Two key areas are used to assess fitness: BMI and body fat percentage.

BMI

The easiest way to get an idea of your body fat percentage is to use the body mass index scale or BMI. Though this does not measure your body fat percentage accurately, it gives you an idea of your body's fatness. This formula shows you the amount of fat your body has in relation to its lean tissue. In most cases, this equation is a fairly accurate indicator of the amount of body fat a person has. To calculate your BMI, divide your weight (in kg) by your height squared (in m). Depending on the result, you can be classified as underweight, normal, overweight or obese. BMI results are not based on a rigid set of numbers because everyone is different. They are based on your sex, age, height and weight. All of these factors are taken into account when calculating a BMI score. For a 15-year-old girl, a BMI index of around 16–17 is normal. As you age, your BMI changes as well. On a broad spectrum, this is what your BMI should be:

20 years: 24–26
30 years: 26–27
40 years: 27–28
50 years: 28–29
60 years: 27–28

The normal ranking changes over time and, around the age of 57, it actually begins to drop again. This simply means there is no magic number. Your BMI tells you your current weight status. Here are the rankings and what they mean:

Below 18.5   : Underweight
18.5–24.9   : Normal
25–29.9   : Overweight
30 and above : Obese

Height has a direct effect on BMI because the taller you are, the more mass you will have. Since there is more mass, the ratio result of body fat will be different from that of someone who is shorter.

Body fat percentage

Measuring body fat percentage is a bit more complicated than using the BMI formula, which is why BMI is so widely used. At a gym or at a dietician's office, you can have your body fat percentage tested with callipers. Callipers are a clamp-like device used to take skin-fold measurements at several places on your body. This method is less accurate than many other body fat measurement tools; however, it is much easier to use than other methods, making it the most commonly used method for measuring body fat percentage.

Body fat percentages in men

Ages 20–39: 8 per cent–19 per cent
Ages 40–59: 11 per cent–21 per cent
Ages 60–79: 13 per cent–24 per cent

Body fat percentages in women

Ages 20–39: 21 per cent–32 per cent
Ages 40–59: 23 per cent–33 per cent
Ages 60–79: 24 per cent–35 per cent

OTHER PARAMETERS

The other parameters people usually ignore while doing a fitness assessment are muscle-and-joint fitness, abdominal strength and flexibility. Knowing your muscle-and-joint strength is important because it will tell you what weight you should start with when you join the gym. Otherwise, it becomes a trial-and-error method. This assessment provides us with valuable information on how well your muscles and joints are functioning to provide movement for day-to-day activities, recreation, and to avoid injury. Muscular strength and endurance allows you to participate in your daily activities without fatigue to your body. Once you know your percentile, you can establish a starting point for exercise and see how you progress with time. Types of muscular endurance assessments include push-ups, half sit-ups and the bench press tests. Once your muscle strength is analysed, you know what your limit is. Also, some trainers push clients into doing more weights than they can handle. That will only result in injury. So do it scientifically and record the weights that you carry every day. That way you will know how much progress you have made. And you will be surprised at how your body is ready to accept challenges that you are not providing.

Flexibility will give you an indication of whether you are suffering from back trouble and tight hamstrings. A lot of people suffer from lower back problems because, let's face it, we are all professional sitters, and this makes our bodies very inflexible. Some people can't even touch their toes. At our gym, we also check if you are flatfooted or have knock knees; such people tend to have big hips. Most trainers don't notice this and make these people only work on their lower bodies, thus injuring their knees even more. Inflexibility around a joint can increase risk of injury. These limitations can affect your everyday activities, such as bending, walking and sitting. Muscles are responsible for flexibility in any part of your body. An increased range of motion around a joint will give you more freedom to move the joint, thus reducing your chance of injury. Types of muscle-and-joint-flexibility assessments include trunk flexion and extension, hip flexion and shoulder flexibility tests.

Abdominal strength is also important for your lower back. If you have a bigger paunch, you are carrying 200 times your weight on your lower back. That is why people with a paunch have lordosis, the spine curving inwards. This pressure on the lower back leads to complications and can cause pain.

Cardiorespiratory endurance or aerobic capacity will measure the amount of oxygen your body uses during a graded exercise test and how your heart responds to the workload that is placed on it during the test. This shows the ability of your heart, lungs and blood vessels to supply sufficient oxygen to the muscles and their capacity to utilize the oxygen to generate energy. In other words, this is an indication of your stamina. When you go to a doctor, you get a blood report that shows your body's whole profile. A fitness assessment does something similar.

DIFFERENT BODY TYPES

People come in all shapes, and the right way to start a workout is by knowing what you are dealing with. Before you start your training and nutrition regimen, it is wise to figure out your body type. Knowing which of these three basic body types you are closest to will help you tailor better your diet and exercise plan and set realistic fitness goals.

Ectomorph body type

Ectomorphs are often below the average weight for their height and have a skinny appearance. Their muscle and bone outlines are usually visible and they normally have low fat and muscle mass. Ectomorphs are thin people whose BMR is always very high. These are people who eat whatever they want and still remain thin, like models. It is impossible for normal people to become ectomorphs without putting their health in serious jeopardy. Ectomorphs tend to have a very high rate of metabolism and often complain of little to no weight gain despite relentless eating. Common ectomorph characteristics include skinny appearance, hyperactivity, fast metabolism, ability to eat whatever they want, small chest and buttocks, difficulty in building muscle, difficulty in gaining weight, low body fat and narrow frame.

Training tips for ectomorphs

- Train heavier with repetitions in the 5–10 range.
- Train each body part once a week.
- Change training routine at least monthly.
- Increase training intensity for each workout. This may mean weights, sets and reps.
- Take longer rest breaks (due to higher weights used).
- Do compound lifts.

Diet tips for ectomorphs

- Eat high-density weight gainers for added calories.
- Try high-density foods such as almonds, avocado or peanut butter.
- Eat at least 50–60 per cent carbohydrates.
- Eat food rich in protein to gain lean muscle.
- Eat slower-burning glycaemic index foods such as beans, corn, oats and pasta.

Endomorph body type

The endomorph body type is the complete opposite of an ectomorph. Such people will usually be larger in appearance with heavier fat accumulation and little muscle definition. They find it hard to drop the excess weight even though they try several diets or workouts. Common endomorph characteristics include large amount of fat accumulation, incessant fatigue, insatiable appetite, inability to lose weight, eating larger meals or several small meals, low muscle definition and larger frame.

Training tips for endomorphs

- Train in the 15+ repetition range.
- Take 30–45-second rest periods between sets.
- Do as much cardio as possible.
- Use moderate poundage. Avoid training with heavy weights and low reps.
- With slower metabolism you won't require as much sleep.
- Training goal is to amp up your metabolism and minimize body fat.

- Change your training programme every second or third workout.

Diet tips for endomorphs

- Portion your meals appropriately—one fist-size equals one serving.
- Eat 30–40 per cent carbohydrates.
- Eat non-processed foods and include whole grains in your diet.
- Eat a lot of vegetables to keep you full.
- Drink plenty of water to keep you full.
- Consume dairy products that are non-fat.
- Skip second helpings and eat slowly.
- Divide your daily caloric intake by 5–6 meals.
- Take in 200–500 calories less than your current calorie intake. You will be walking away from each meal feeling slightly hungry.
- Eliminate soft drinks and alcohol from your diet.

Mesomorph body type

Everyone recognizes a mesomorph, because that's what we all want. Mesomorphs are somewhere between ectomorphs and endomorphs and display characteristics of both. They have a larger frame like endomorphs, but a low body fat percentage like ectomorphs. You could say this is the body type everybody aspires to. Mesomorphs are blessed people. They barely exercise and are still always in the best shape. All I can say is that God loves them more and has endowed them with superior genes. And so we come to the matter of genetics. Genetics does not come into play when you say that you are overweight because your mother and father are overweight. That just means the whole family is eating wrong.

Common mesomorph characteristics are symmetrical build, being naturally muscular and strong, good shoulder-to-waist ratio, wide shoulders, small waist, low body fat, building muscle easily, ability to burn fat easily and eating in moderation.

Training tips for mesomorphs

- Train in the 8–12 repetition rep range.
- 30-second–1-minute rest periods between sets.
- Alternate 3–4 weeks of high-intensity training

with several weeks of low-intensity workouts to promote growth and strength and prevent burnout.
- Do enough cardio to stay lean, but not a lot.
- Regularly alternate intensity techniques in your workouts: partial reps, forced reps, descending sets, compound sets and pre-exhaustion.

Diet tips for mesomorphs

- Keep carbohydrate intake moderately high—about 60 per cent of total calories. Choose vegetables, rice, low-fat beans, lentils and pasta.
- Limit fat—stay lean with a diet containing 10–20 per cent fat.
- Portion meals by balling up your fist—that's the size of one portion.
- Break meals into 5–6 smaller meals throughout the day.
- Eat enough calories to gain lean muscle mass.

POINTS TO PONDER

- The easiest way to get an idea of your body fat percentage is to use the body mass index scale or BMI. Though this does not measure your body fat percentage accurately, it gives you an idea of your body's fatness.

- Our fitness assessment is a one-hour test where we check a person's body fat percentage, measurements, cardiorespiratory capacity, muscle strength, muscle endurance, flexibility, grip strength and abdominal strength.

- If you feel good about the way you look, you will automatically be in a good frame of mind and ultimately have good health. And that is how you will be able to handle the stresses of life.

Chapter 2

Myths about Fitness

IT'S EASY TO FALL INTO the trap. A workout friend passes along an exercise tip. You look at his body and figure it must be true. And then you pass it on to several other friends. But, in the world of fitness, there are plenty of myths, some of which may be keeping you from getting the best and safest workout. Some myths are just harmless half-truths, but many can be harmful. They can cause discomfort during workouts and, sometimes, even lead to injury. There is a lot of fitness information out there—some reliable, some not. So it is important to take such advice with a grain of salt. If you don't understand something, ask a qualified fitness professional for advice. Sticking to the truth of these myths will keep you healthy and injury-free.

One reason why myths get started is that we all react to exercise differently. So what is true for one person may not be true for another. That is why you have to find what is true for you. But there are still some fitness myths that just need busting.

What you don't know about fitness can hurt you and interfere with your fitness goals. For a safer workout with awesome results, get your fitness facts straight.

Myth: You only need to exercise if you have weight to lose

Fact: Ever heard the term 'skinny fat'? According to researchers at Mayo Clinic, US, over half of so-called normal-weight adults fall under this category. It has been defined as having more than 30 per cent body fat for women or 20 per cent for men. Too much body fat puts you at the same disease risk as an obese person—you're just more likely to suffer from undetected diabetes. But don't try to diet your way out of this one—it can actually make the problem worse, since dieters who cut calories alone tend to lose more lean muscle (in effect increasing your percentage of body fat). It's time to get moving, skinny.

Myth: Size zero

Fact: I blame a certain actor and the media for propagating this myth. Size zero is a clothing size, not your figure. And this so-called size zero can be attained if you starve and exercise to within an inch of your life. It serves no purpose and is only designed to make women feel bad about their bodies. Size zero means you are bordering on anorexia, and that is neither healthy nor beautiful.

Myth: Fat can be spot-reduced

Fact: This concept is called spot reduction and, unfortunately, it doesn't burn fat. When you lose weight, you cannot really choose the area in which the reduction will occur. Your body predetermines which fat stores it will use up. In a study published in the *Journal of Strength and Conditioning Research*, eleven people completed a twelve-week exercise programme to train a single leg. Even though they only trained on one side, they lost almost the same amount of body fat in each leg—and burned even more body fat above the waist. No, doing butt crunches will not get rid of the fat in your rear, and doing sit-ups will not help lose the extra flab in your belly. Your body burns fat on an even keel.

Myth: Eat less often to lose weight

Fact: The best weight-loss diet plan is to eat no less than 1200 calories per day if you are a woman, or 1800 if you are a man, over 5–6 small meals. When your body is starved, it slows down your metabolism, so less food will cause a bigger impact on your body weight. Eat the same amount of wholesome foods, but eat more often to keep that metabolism rate high.

Myth: Lifting heavy weights bulks you up

Fact: Weight training actually helps women slim down instead of bulk up, since women have much lower testosterone levels than men. Women who lift a challenging weight for 8 reps burn nearly twice as many calories as women who do 15 reps with lighter dumb-bells, according to a study published in *Medicine and Science in Sports and Exercise*.

In a study at Central Michigan University, US, researchers had women train with one arm doing only a few reps of a heavy weight and the other doing more reps with a lighter weight (both lifting an equivalent number of pounds). Surprise: The arms that lifted heavy weights got stronger, but gained no more size than the arms lifting the lower weights. Ladies, weight training is very good for you. It will lead to increased metabolism and strength, lower risk of osteoporosis and a smaller waistline!

MYTH: AB EXERCISES WILL GIVE YOU A FLAT STOMACH

Fact: The only way to get a flat stomach is to strip away the fat around the midsection. This is accomplished by doing cardio/aerobic exercise to burn calories, weight training to increase metabolism, and following a proper diet. Abdominal exercises will help to build muscle in your midsection, but you will never see the muscle definition unless the fat in this area is stripped away. You should create a workout that includes both cardio exercises and weight training. This will decrease your overall body fat content, including the area around your midsection.

Myth: If you don't sweat, you are not working out hard enough

Fact: Sweating is not an indicator of exertion. It is your body's way of cooling itself. It is possible to burn a significant number of calories without breaking a sweat.

Myth: As long as you feel okay when you are working out, you are not overdoing it

Fact: One of the biggest mistakes people make when starting or returning to an exercise programme is doing too much too soon. We do that because we feel fine while we are working out. But you would not really feel you overdid it until a day or two later. No matter how good you feel when you return to exercising after an absence, you should never try to duplicate how much or how hard you worked in the past. Even if you don't feel it right then, you will feel it in time.

Myth: Sports drinks are beneficial

Fact: Drinks like Gatorade are good for recovering from long exercises or sports. The problem is, most people only have time for an hour or less of cardio. Consuming 130 calories worth of sugar after an ordinary workout may just cancel out your caloric burn.

Myth: No pain, no gain

Fact: Exercise should not be painful. At the height of your workout, you should be sweating and breathing hard. You should not be so out of breath that you cannot answer a question. That's how you know you are working at a good level. It's important to distinguish between muscle fatigue—what people at my gym call 'the burn'—and muscle pain, which is sharp and uncomfortable when you move. Pain is your body's way of telling you that you are doing something wrong. Listen to your body. If it is in pain, stop.

Myth: You can't build muscle with vegetable

Fact: To build muscle, you need three consistent elements: stimulus from exercise, calories, and nutrients to support muscle building and recovery. Vegetables are filled with slow-digesting carbs, minerals and vitamins. They are like grains, but with fewer calories. If you eat enough calories and complete proteins, you will gain muscle. Overeating is anabolic in itself and that is why stuffing yourself all day will help gain muscle. However, all that eating will also lead to unwanted-fat gain. By including vegetables as the carb source in your diet, you will be able to stay leaner, feel fuller and be healthier while you build muscle. The only time this myth is actually true is when you fail to meet your caloric requirement. Without enough calories, you will not be able to build muscle. Moreover, you cannot hope to build muscle if you only eat vegetables. You need food that gives you complete proteins. So, if you are a vegetarian, balance your veggies with protein from nuts, dairy products or soy.

Myth: Carbs are bad

Fact: If you want to gain muscle, you are going to need carbs. If you take them out completely, you will burn more body fat during training perhaps, but you cannot possibly keep it up for long. Carbs are fuel for intense workouts; fats are not. You need a minimum amount of carbs to ensure that your brain functions properly. The brain needs glucose to work. Your body can be ketonic and use fatty acids to fuel your muscles, but your brain simply cannot.

Myth: A woman's metabolism slows down after the age of 30. After that, she is doomed to be fat

Fact: The reason metabolism slows down as we get older is a combination of lower hormone levels and less athletic activity. If you don't work out and eat healthy food, you will get out of shape. An untrained body becomes even more evident as you get older.

Myth: If a product has zero calories, you can have as much as you want

Fact: Zero-calorie syrups, jams, dressings, etc. are not really no-cal. Products can be advertised as being no-cal if they have fewer than 5 calories per servings. In reality, most of these products have about 5 calories per serving, so if you are going to down the whole bottle, you will actually end up having more than 60 calories. Although that doesn't seem like a lot, adding 60 calories of meagre nutrition to your diet won't do much to help your fitness plan.

Myth: Running is bad for your knees

Fact: A Stanford University study found that older runners' knees were no less healthy than those of people who do not run. But while pounding the pavement is safer on the joints than contact sports like football, it is not totally harmless. Women are four to six times as likely to be at risk of serious knee injuries from running as men, because they tend to have an imbalance in the strength ratio between their quadriceps and hamstrings. That is why experts recommend doing a total body strength workout at least twice a week in addition to your regular jogs, to build up the muscles that support your knees. This will enhance your running experience and also reduce your chances of getting injured.

Myth: Protein shakes are great for weight loss

Fact: This won't work. Most shakes are a mix of cheap protein, vitamins, sugar and colouring agents. It's not that they are inherently bad for you, but that they are not very filling. Wholesome foods have more fibre and take up more stomach volume, which keeps you feeling satisfied. They are also more difficult to digest, and hence use up more energy and keep the metabolism up. But if you really have to drink them, look for high-end whey protein and add some fats like nuts or oil to increase satiety.

Myth: Eat only egg white and not the yolk

Fact: Egg yolks have been having a bad reputation for a long time—they are supposedly bad for your cholesterol. But eggs will not affect your cholesterol balance unless they are fried in butter and served with bacon. In fact, a study by the University of Connecticut found that the fat in the yolk helped to reduce LDL—the bad cholesterol. The yolk contains most of the vitamins and minerals in the egg, plus half the protein. Since an egg-white-only breakfast is nearly fat-free, it will cause a significant insulin spike and promote hunger cravings as well as energy swings later in the day.

Myth: You shouldn't exercise during your period

Fact: This is absolute rubbish! Menstruation is a normal function. Your period is not a disability; you can do anything during your period that you can do when you are not menstruating. In fact, exercise releases endorphins—the body's natural painkiller. This means that light workouts will reduce period cramps and pains. If you have heavy flow, don't exercise like you do every day. Something lighter will do you good. Regular aerobic exercise helps relieve PMS, and exercise can even simply be a way to take your mind off the irritability and pain that can come with a woman's time of the month.

> ### POINTS TO PONDER
>
> - Size zero is a clothing size, not your figure.
> - Exercise is never painful.
> - Your period is not a disability; you can do anything during your period that you can do when you are not menstruating.
> - Have a fitness professional chart out a workout schedule for you.

Chapter 3

Starting Out

FEW PEOPLE IN THIS WORLD are born loving the gym. But what generally separates people who like working out from those who don't is pretty simple: fitness.

Working out sucks when you are not in shape. But the good news is that you don't need to become a pro to get to a place where exercise is no longer a pain. Just like while learning to cook, once you reach a level that does not make you want to pull out your hair, exercise stops feeling bad and starts feeling good. And just like with cooking, the only way to get there is to just do it. If you are just starting a workout programme, your goal should not be to lose weight. The first step is getting to a fitness level where you no longer hate exercise. For that, all you need is consistency.

When I talk about how to start moving towards a fitness regimen, I talk about the need to change your lifestyle. You have to learn to manage your lifestyle, because you cannot be on a low-fat diet every day of your life! You cannot *not* eat the food you love for the rest of your life! You cannot stop consuming sweets and fried food. Everybody knows that moderation is the key. But you have to actually put it into effect. So how do we at Leena Mogre's Fitness go about it? We go about it by making small changes in your lifestyle.

That is why we stress that lifestyle management is the key to your fitness. It means you have to start including fitness in your daily routine. It can be a short walk, or it can be dancing, swimming, cycling or going to the gym. This is a start. This has to be an activity you are picking up because you love it. There are people who say, 'I'm not the gym kind, but I love dancing.' So do that! There are a lot of overweight people who have taken up CrossFit. Many of them get injured because they do not get their fitness assessed. And then they blame exercise for their injuries. It is actually the other way round. Because you don't get an assessment done, your injuries are going to rise. Say you are overweight and you take up a dance class that involves a lot of jumps. You will surely have knee and back injuries in the long run. To avoid that, the best thing you can do for yourself is first get a fitness assessment. In the assessment, we look for flexibility, endurance, strength, cardiorespiratory endurance and, of course, your BMI and body fat percentage. Get your blood tests done—cholesterol, triglyceride, diabetes, HDL:LDL ratio and other things that the doctor will point out. Only when all this is done should you go ahead with your fitness programme. A lot of gyms do not do this sort of assessment. They just put you on some electronic machine and get a printout. But nothing is done about the numbers that show up.

A fitness assessment test will encompass your entire fitness profile. So you are not only working for fat or weight loss. There are other areas you need to look out for as well. If you don't improve your flexibility, you will have back and knee injuries in the long run. A lot of people go to the free-weight areas in the gym and start pushing weights, and the gyms don't bother to correct them. The worst thing I have observed is that gyms tell celebs, who know only their own bodies, to give tips. The celebrities do not know if the person they are advising is suffering from a serious disease like diabetes or has heart trouble. What we can hence conclude is that what works for you will not work for someone else. Each body is different. And you need to assess *your* body.

Get your food in order

If you are about to work out five hours a week, fantastic! The good news about this is, for the other 163 hours, you can be as lazy as you like. But diet is a 24/7 thing. It is a good idea to start thinking about it now, along with your new-found exercise regimen.

The next step is to get a diet and a lifestyle assessment that is tailor-made for you. Eating right and exercising are organically connected. Once you get into it, working out can give you the same rush that a package of Oreos can. But there will be points where a 300-calorie burning workout session will lead you to eating a 500-calorie piece of cheesecake.

Unfortunately, it does not work like that. When you start exercising, you must monitor your food intake as well.

Eating junk will make it harder to exercise. It is not just a weight thing—it is about how you feel. If you are serious about working out, let that attitude reflect in your diet as well. You will feel a lot more prepared to take on that run after a meal full of vitamins and nutrients than you would if you forked down preservatives and chemical additives.

Without gyms knowing what kind of job you do, what kind of activities you do, what kinds of food you like and dislike, or when you wake up and go to sleep, even the best diet in the world will not work for you. Another thing that bothers me a lot is when people borrow diets that their friends have been following just so they can save some money. That makes absolutely no sense. 'What diet are you on? Why don't I try it?' These are questions I hear all around me. I am appalled that people just experiment with random diets without knowing if that particular diet is right for them and their body type. You friend's body is very different from yours. The reason she is gaining weight is why you are doing the same now. So please stop this and find out what *your* body needs.

What time do you wake up? When do you go to sleep? What do you eat for breakfast and dinner? How often do you eat out? How often do you party? Life is full of celebrations. You are not going to sit at home your entire life just because you are on a diet, right? And then you complain about healthy food being boring. That is why people do not want to adopt a fit lifestyle. That is because in front of them they can only see lettuce leaves or salads or boiled legumes and pulses. They are denying themselves drinks and sweets and the other foods that make life wonderful. That is why most of us try our best to stay away from a fitness regimen.

The next step is to start correcting what you are doing wrong. Maybe your meal times need to be corrected. Everyone around me these days talks of just one thing—'I should not eat carbs after 6 p.m.' Now, that is just ridiculous. This is why domestic fights start after 7 p.m. Because your brain craves carbs, and when it does not get them, you get irritable. So get your food plan sorted by a qualified nutritionist. Do not make these decisions for yourself.

Get your basics right

Not only do you have to possess the ability and the machinery, you also have to have some idea of what you are doing. Here are some basic terms you should start including in your vocabulary:

Set: This term is used during weight training. It is the same exercise repeated a specific number of times. So when you hear someone say, 'I did 3 sets of bench press on Monday', you know what they mean.

Repetition or rep: This is the number within the set. For instance, 'I did 2 sets of 10 reps each.'

Warm-up: This is not the same as stretching. Warming up is doing very light exercise, like walking before a run. It increases blood flow and heats up your muscles. You will break into a sweat and your heartbeat will quicken. Stretching should come in at the end of your workout. Never stretch on a cold body.

Cool down: Never do a full stop; your body will have no idea what happened. Instead, go at a reduced speed for whatever activity you were doing, hence telling your body that it is almost time to relax. Stretching is often part of a cool down. This is to ensure that your body process comes back to normal.

Why you need a personal trainer

Workouts will differ at every level. They will differ for a person with back problems, knee problems, spondilycis, diabetes, etc. A lot of people shy away from coming to the gym, citing these problems. But these problems will only get more intense if you do not change your lifestyle and come to the gym. But why the gym and why not just go for a walk or dance it away? Because, in the gym, you are monitored by trainers. I always tell newcomers at my gym not to shy away from hiring a personal trainer. But their answer always is, 'Let me become a regular gym goer. Then I'll hire a personal trainer.' That makes absolutely no sense. When you hire a personal trainer right from the beginning, you'll become regular with your exercises. Work with a trainer for three months and then you can choose to do it alone. Each workout with the personal trainer will be tailored for you to get maximum benefits without overdoing it. They will also support you in fitting other activities into your life in a manageable way. What works for one person may not work for another when it comes to choosing an exercise programme. A personal trainer will develop the most effective programme for you based on your fitness evaluation results and personal goals. He will ensure that your form and technique are correct from the beginning and will help you to be consistent with your workout; he will call you up when you don't show up. Also, the fact that you have paid money means you will stick with the regimen, if only to ensure you get your money's worth. A personal trainer will keep you from getting stuck in a rut. He or she is a great choice if you need some variety in your workouts. A trainer will constantly engage you with new challenges and ways to train. He or she can bring a fresh perspective and new ideas to challenge both your body and your mind. Even if you just do a few sessions or meet every few weeks, you will find it refreshing to have new workouts and new exercise equipment to try out. It is true that feeling good makes you look good.

If you have any specific issues like heart disease,

old injuries, etc., working with an experienced trainer can help you find a programme to help heal injuries and avoid any further problems. Not only can your personal trainer help you achieve your health and fitness goals, he or she can provide you with positive feedback on your performance and build your confidence to take on new challenges.

I have also seen a lot of people pick up a game like badminton or squash to get started in fitness. But after a few months, I see them wearing knee caps or waist—which I call waste—belts because they were not fit to play the game. Become fit to play games; don't play games to become fit.

It takes around one and a half months for a person to form any habit. So forty-five days is what it will take you to change your lifestyle. And if you make exercising a habit, you will start loving it soon enough. Then you will stop searching for excuses to miss exercising.

This way, even if you make small changes in your life, the results will show faster. This makes more sense than making drastic changes to your diet. In such instances, the dietician will ask you to buy expensive things and when you are sick of the diet in a few days, all that stuff will go to waste. Make changes in the time you have breakfast or a mid-morning snack. Maybe you can have an apple every day, or have three different foods in a day, or snack on a handful of almonds you have kept in your desk cupboard. But you have to start by exercising at least three times a week, if not every day.

At the gym, for a monthly fee, you will have access to a room full of equipment, classes and a trainer. Everything you could possibly need will be at one place. It can't get easier than that.

POINTS TO PONDER

- Lifestyle management is the key to your fitness. That means you have to start by making changes in your habits and including fitness in your daily routine.

- When you hire a personal trainer right from the beginning, you will become regular with your exercises. Work with a trainer for three months and then you can choose to do it alone.

> - I am appalled that people just experiment with random diets without knowing if it is right for them and their body type. Your friend's body is very different from yours.

Chapter 4

Working Out at Your Fitness Level

How do you want to get fit?

PEOPLE EXERCISE FOR DIFFERENT REASONS. Perhaps you do weight training to build up your strength, yoga to relax, or play a game to improve your fitness. Each of these benefits your body in a different way. Different types of exercise emphasize different elements of physical fitness. Well-balanced workout regimens include different types of exercise to help you avoid injury and develop or maintain overall physical fitness. You may perform different types of exercise in varying proportions, depending on your goals. Here are a few common programmes that people follow.

Walking

Most people walk at some point in the day. Increasing the distance you walk is easier than you think. You can make it a social affair by joining a local walking group. And you don't need to have a fit body to walk. Just put on a good pair of shoes and hit the road. Regular walking is good for you because it strengthens the heart and lungs, increasing your overall fitness. Together with diet and other exercise plans, it can also help to lose weight and tone up muscles. Walking can improve muscle endurance as well as muscle strength, especially in the lower body. It is good for your bones and helps boost circulation.

Fitness level required: Beginner

Running

Anybody can pick up running. Running makes more demands on your body than walking. The benefits are greater, but so are the risks in terms of injury. When you can walk briskly for 20 minutes continuously, you can try to walk–jog. Walk for a minute and then jog for a minute, alternating the speeds throughout your session. It helps if you have a running instructor. Running bolsters your cartilage by increasing oxygen flow and flushing out toxins, and by strengthening the ligaments around your joints. But be sure to learn the techniques of running and do required sport-specific strength training at least twice a week or there is a possibility of injury.

Fitness level required: Beginner

Cycling

Most car or rickshaw trips that you take can easily be covered on a bicycle. Cycling works your lower body and cardiovascular system. Start slowly and increase your sessions gradually. As with jogging or walking, you can ride with friends, family or a cycling group. But as you advance and love cycling more and more every day, I'm sure you will need a bicycle that has gears. So get trained to use that. Contrary to perception, cycling is not just good for your legs. It builds strength in a holistic manner since every single part of the body is involved in cycling. It is also known to build stamina, improve the health of your heart, reduce stress and improve coordination. But beware of lower back injuries. Do sport-specific strength training twice a week.

Fitness level required: Beginner

Dancing

Dance is becoming increasingly popular. Studios have never been fuller, with classes ranging from ballroom dancing to salsa. It improves your balance and your coordination. It is suitable for people of all ages, shapes and sizes. But inform your instructor beforehand if you suffer from knee problems because dancing can be hard on them. Check if the flooring is made of suspended wood. Dancing can give you a great mind–body workout. Researchers are learning that regular physical activity, in general, can help keep your body, including your brain, healthy as you age. Plus, it's a sure-fire way to get a toned body.

Fitness level required: Beginner

Belly dancing, however, requires an intermediate level of fitness because if your core is not strong, you will get hurt.

Kick-boxing

Kick-boxing has become increasingly popular in recent times. Like other forms of aerobic exercise, kick-boxing is a terrific way for you to burn calories. According to Harvard Medical School, a 70-kg person burns around 372 calories during a 30-minute kick-boxing class. Heavier people, people who work out more intensely and people who work out for longer periods will burn even more calories. A lot of people pick this up to lose weight, but you need to be monitored very well. If you have knee or back problems, stay away at a good distance.

Fitness level required: Beginner

Functional training

You might be toned and fit, but are you ready to lift

your child out of the car or carry a 30-kg suitcase down the stairs? Functional training focuses on making your body strong enough to do real-life activities in real-life positions, not just lifting a certain amount of weight in an idealized posture instructed by the trainer. It is about training all the muscles to work together rather than isolating them to work independently.

Fitness level required: All levels

At the beginner's level, avoid all plyometric workouts like jump squats, for example. Then you can progress to the next—intermediate—level.

Circuit training

Circuit training is a fast-paced class in which you do one exercise for 30 seconds to 5 minutes and then move on to another exercise. It increases your strength and aerobic fitness and burns lots of calories. Stretch before you start with circuit training. Keep in mind that when you are doing any kind of stretching workouts, you must differentiate between pain and the feel-good pain of stretching. If you stretch beyond what your body is ready for, you can get a muscle spasm or tear.

Fitness level required: Can be adjusted to any level

Spinning

Spinning is a replication of outdoor cycling that is done indoors on specially designed stationary bikes. With upbeat music setting the tone, the instructor guides the class. You may burn as much as 500 calories during a spinning workout of 45 minutes, which is a huge amount when compared to other types of exercises. It is also a great way to tone your core muscles, buttocks and thighs.

Fitness level required: Beginner

Beginners should be comfortable spinning because if you know how to ride a bike, you will be able to grasp the technique. Plus, you can follow at your own pace. You can sit when the group is standing or ease up the tension when it is too tough for you to pedal.

If you have high blood pressure, be sure to inform your instructor. If you have any health problems, you need to do heart-rate-monitor training so you know at what heart rate you are spinning.

CrossFit

Short and very intense, CrossFit workouts combine gymnastics, sprints, plyometrics and Olympic weightlifting for an all-round challenge to your body. CrossFitters see results fast, according to a study in the *Journal of Strength and Conditioning Research*. After just ten weeks of high-intensity training, including lifts such as the squat, deadlift, clean, snatch and overhead press performed as quickly as possible, the men and women in the study cut their body fat by an average of 4 per cent.

Fitness level required: Intermediate

You require at least intermediate level of fitness, or you will definitely get injured.

Bootcamp

Bootcamp includes interval training, body resistance training, athletic drills, obstacle courses and sport-specific training. It involves bursts of high-intensity work, such as resisted movements against a specific force, alternated with periods of recovery.

The programme is simple, but challenges you to push the boundaries of your endurance in order to achieve your fitness goals.

Fitness level required: Beginner

But if you are overweight, be careful because you might injure your knees and shins.

Power yoga

The concept of power yoga has been getting some buzz, but a lot of people are confused as to what the practice actually entails. Power yoga is an intense workout that will make you sweat. A traditional Ashtanga practice follows the same series of poses and makes you hold each pose for five breaths before moving on to a Vinyasa. Power yoga classes move with an even faster rhythm. It is great for strength training and aerobic fitness.

Fitness level required: Beginner

You can start off at the beginner's level, but, if you are overweight, avoid a lot of Suryanamaskars because it will ruin your knees and lower back. Be sure to stretch for at least 5 minutes towards the end.

DIFFERENT LEVELS OF FITNESS

There was a time when you were either fit or not. But now, with the array of exercises to suit your every mood, you have to know how strong your body is before you embark on a let's-get-fit regimen. Here are the broad definitions that most professionals adhere to.

Beginner: If you do not do any form of exercise, you are at the beginner's level of fitness.

Intermediate: At least one year of continuous workouts means you have this level of fitness.

Advanced: More than two years of exercising means you are ready for almost any fitness challenge.

Elite: Over five years of keeping yourself fit means you can experiment with any level of exercise. But you will still need to get assessed for whatever routine you plan to take up.

POINTS TO PONDER

- Well-balanced workout regimens include different types of exercise to help you avoid injury and develop or maintain overall physical fitness.

- Functional training focuses on making your body strong enough to do real-life activities in real-life positions, not just lifting a certain amount of weight in an idealized posture on a machine.

- Cycling is not just good for your legs. It builds strength in a holistic manner since every single part of the body is involved in the exercise.

CHAPTER 5

SUSTAINING YOUR WORKOUT

THERE ARE PLENTY OF DIETS, fads, workout and weight-loss programmes out there. Many of them are questionable, while others can be trusted. Ultimately it all comes down to some pretty simple concepts. With our hectic lives, it is not easy to stick to a plan. But you can motivate yourself to sustain your health goal and stay in a healthy routine for life.

Don't overdo it

An extremely common mistake is starting everything together. People join a gym, go on a diet, join a spinning class or start jogging. They overdo things right at the beginning. What happens then is that they fall sick because their body is not used to so many changes at one go. And then they just drop out. It does not help that most gyms don't even have fitness assessment or a sustained plan to start off, depending on the fitness level of the client. As I had mentioned earlier, it takes about forty-five days to make anything a habit. So it becomes the trainer's or gym's duty as well to motivate the client to be regular in those forty-five days. In those one-and-a-half months, if you start exercising even three days a week, it will become a habit. Then your body looks forward to exercise and you start to push yourself. This can happen only when you start off slowly. That way you have not made the mistake of jumping into the whole thing without thinking about it rationally.

SET SMALL GOALS

A sure-fire way to lose your motivation to exercise very quickly is to start out with a killing workout. If you set yourself tough goals in the beginning, you probably won't achieve them and will then become discouraged. The key is to set smaller and easier goals and work your way up. So if you have to lose 25 kg, stop trying to lose 10 kg in two months. Your goal should be to lose 1 kg a week because a long-term plan will help to keep the weight off. And it is important to concentrate on body fat percentage rather than your weight. Body fat percentage is measured using fat callipers, which are available in all gyms. Many dieticians tell their clients not to work out and avoid weight training and to just go for a walk. That is because they only care about showing their clients on the weighing scale that they have lost weight. In fact, in the first month of dieting, the weighing scale may actually show more because your lean muscle tissue has just started building up. And muscle weighs more than fat. It is important to remember that muscle does not get converted to fat and vice versa. That is why I never call it weight loss, it is always fat loss. A lot of people say that they are dropping inches, but their weight stays the same. So please don't get obsessed with the weighing scale.

MAKE IT A LIFESTYLE CHOICE

If you are exercising simply because you feel like

you should or because you got breathless going up a flight of stairs or because you saw a picture of a school friend who looks better than you, it isn't going to stick. The desire to stay healthy has to outweigh all of those external motivators. A lot of workout programmes never get off the ground because people are trying to schedule their workouts like they schedule trips to the dentist. It cannot be viewed as an inconvenience that you are just trying to squeeze into your day. You have to have a mindset that says, 'This is who I am now. This is part of my life.' If you can get to that point, you are well on your way.

Get a logbook

Always keep a logbook for your diet and your workouts. When you record what you have eaten on a particular day, you will realize your mistake on your own. Even a small sweet you put in your mouth has to be noted down. That is how you learn lifestyle management and how to discipline yourself. I also suggest you buy a dress or a pair of jeans two sizes smaller and keep it on the right side of your cupboard. So whenever you open your cupboard you see the dress you want to fit into and try it on regularly. That is the best motivation. I have a 25-year-old pair of jeans and I still fit into them. The minute I realize they are tight or I can't pull the zip up, I know that my body fat percentage has gone up. This pair is the best indicator of my weight and the shape of my body. That is how I realize that I have become unfit. I do not call it putting on weight; I call it being unfit because if you are fit, you will not put on weight.

Remember a good exercise experience

A study conducted by the US National Library of Medicine found that you can use memory to enhance motivation. Study participants who described a positive memory of exercise were not only more motivated to exercise but also actually exercised more over the next week than those who were not prompted to remember. So stash your medal from the Mumbai or Delhi half-marathon when you ran your personal record with your exercise clothes, or pack your power-walking playlist with songs you love to dance to. The good memories may pave the way to a good sweat.

Wear workout clothes you like

Buy training gear that motivates you to go to the gym every day. Don't wear clothes that are loose or have dull colours. Colourful, cheerful, right gear for your workout means you look forward to wearing that to the gym. If you buy tight gear, you will see where fat is popping out when you are in the gym in front of the mirror. Visual impact makes a lot of sense for you to get into the groove because you will start seeing the reduction in fat as well. Many of my male clients tell me they want a lean build, not big biceps like a bodybuilder. But when they put on even one inch, you should see how their sleeves are rolled up a bit. Also, don't get comfortable in loose clothes. Wearing loose clothes like anarkalis does not hide your fat. In fact, it adds to the bulk. Break out of your comfort zone; you will be surprised at what you can do.

SURROUND YOURSELF WITH POSITIVITY

When you need motivation, the worst thing that you can do is compare yourself to others or be around people who put you down. The good news is there are plenty of people who are looking for motivation as well. So find these people and work together to accomplish something. Plus, you will make friends for life.

READ SUCCESS STORIES

Though you might think you will be jealous, you would be surprised by how inspiring other people's stories can be. Reading others' success stories will make you think, 'If she can do it, so can I.' And that is exactly how it works—you see these normal people who took on marvellous feats and came out ahead. There is no reason to believe you can't be next.

PUSH YOUR BODY

Your body can accept a lot of challenges. It is you who is not challenging your body, who is allowing your body to decay. A lot of people who go for walks do the same 5 km or 7 km every day and I don't see any change in their bodies. This is where the intensity of your workout starts to matter. Start increasing the intensity, so you know how much progress you have made and can feel proud of how far you have come. This also keeps you motivated. When you increase the intensity of your workout, you will see a marked difference in your body. And when you see that difference, you will want to increase the intensity even more. That is the best way to sustain your workout. This is also why hiring a personal trainer makes sense. One of my clients runs a tattoo parlour and was the laziest person I had met in a while. I insisted that she hire a trainer, and even though she always protested, saying she did not want the stress of one, she is now very happy with the deal. Today she works out even on a Sunday. However, the gym should be responsible for giving everyone a schedule even if they have not opted for a personal trainer.

Don't work out next to the fittest person at the gym

A study published in the *International Journal of Eating Disorders* examined how your fellow gym goers affect your workout. Researchers hung out around the lateral pull-down machine at a US college gym. When a woman started using it, an extremely fit female member of the research team started using the adjacent machine. Half the time, she wore a tank top and shorts. The other half of the time, she wore pants with extra thigh padding and a baggy sweatshirt. What happened? Women working out next to her when she was wearing the tank top used their machine for a shorter amount of time than usual. By contrast, women working out next to her when dressed in a baggy sweatshirt exercised longer and did not suffer the same hit to their body image. What does this mean for women? Run on a treadmill behind a 19-year-old and you will probably leave sooner, feeling bad about yourself. Run on a treadmill behind an average-looking person and you are likely to leave after a good workout with your body image intact.

Don't motivate yourself by thinking about flabby abs

Most of us often motivate ourselves to exercise by thinking about our appearance. But it turns out this approach backfires. A study by National Institutes of Health found that frequent exercise goes along with a positive body image, which was defined as appreciating your body, focusing on how it feels, and being satisfied with what it can do. But in the case of gym goers who were only trying to look hot, all three components of positive body image weakened no matter how much they exercised. So consider turning your focus to something other than your thighs and tummy.

Mix it up

Another thing you can focus on is keeping your workouts fresh and inventive. Try not to follow a set programme for days and weeks so you don't get bored. People get too structured in their training programmes when they just don't know what to do. So choose exercises you like and keep them fluctuating. Then find some cardio modes you like. Biking, cycling, running, swimming, whatever you like. Keep it fresh and have some fun. The more fun you have, the less your weight loss feels like work.

Stop thinking of yourself as lazy

Think of yourself as someone who exercises, or someone who is healthy, or whatever exercise-friendly word you would like to use. The human mind goes to great lengths, sometimes unconsciously, to be consistent with how we perceive ourselves to be. So thinking of yourself as a stressed-out person creates a self-fulfilling prophecy with little room for exercise. But thinking of yourself as a really busy, healthy person might be just the tweak your mindset needs.

Be regular

Regular training will help you be successful in your fitness efforts. By regular training, I mean that you should be training at least three or four days per week. That means at least 45–60 minutes of hard, intense training using resistance training and hard cardiovascular efforts. This also means that you fill the rest of the days with steady exercise for about an hour each day. Basically, you should be moving your muscles at least six or seven days a week. But what about the rest day, you ask me? Sure, you can take a rest day. But that does not mean you shouldn't be moving around that day. Even on a rest day you can take a short walk in the park or clean your house. The point is to do some sort of activity.

Reward yourself

After each exercise session, take a few minutes to relish the good feelings that exercise gives you. This type of internal reward can help you make a long-term commitment to regular exercise. External rewards can help, too. When you reach a longer-range goal, treat yourself to a new pair of walking shoes and the like.

Don't let your period stop you

Women have this huge misconception that they

should not work out during their period. If that were true, every female trainer would take off four days every month. If you have very heavy flow, just do some light walking. It has been scientifically proven that working out during your period helps regularize your menstrual cycle. This prevents PMS and the mood swings that come along with it because all your anger and frustration is taken out while exercising.

Don't be too hard on yourself

Life is full of obstacles. Unexpected illness and setbacks are bound to happen. Don't let a few missed workouts turn into a month of unfulfilled resolutions. If you miss a workout, pick yourself up and move on. Don't design your workout plan with the expectation that it will go exactly the way you drew it up. As long as you have the will to stick to it, you are going to progress towards your goals. Everybody has unforeseen circumstances and everybody has moments of weakness, days of fatigue, soreness and laziness. Do not view them as failures. Just get back on to the right path as soon as you can.

POINTS TO PONDER

- Your goal should be to lose 1 kg a week because a long-term plan will help to keep the weight off.

- Your body can accept a lot of challenges. It is you who is not challenging your body, who is allowing your body to decay.

- Do not design your workout plan with the expectation that it will go exactly the way you drew it up. As long as you have the will to stick to it, you are going to progress towards your goals.

Chapter 6

Fad Diets

I DON'T LIKE THE WORD 'diet'. I'd rather people say that they are substituting good food for bad food, that they are trying to change their lifestyle. However, your food choices each day affect your health—how you feel today, tomorrow and in the future. Good nutrition and the right food are important for a healthy lifestyle. Combined with physical activity, your diet can help you to reach and maintain a healthy weight, reduce your risk of heart disease and promote your overall health.

One of the best ways to do that is to have a dietician in your life—someone who is there with you every step of the way, who tells you where you are going wrong (and trust me, you are) and why you need to make that change. There are no shortcuts to weight loss or muscle gain. It has to be a constant effort to change your lifestyle for the better. You need to meet your dietician regularly. You have to consult him or her for even seemingly small things, even inform where you are going to eat that day. So if you are going to eat Mughlai food in a restaurant, he or she will tell you what you should and should not eat there.

The best thing is to make small changes in your lifestyle that you can manage. It may take a little while to reach the fitness level you want, but it will give you lifelong and long-life results. Normally, I never tell my clients about diet first. I want them to start with workouts because jumping into both at the same time will be too much, and they will just drop out.

Changing your diet should be an enjoyable exercise. You should want to eat good food, should love the good food you eat, be disciplined to eat in moderation. I love sweets and ice creams, so I understand how difficult it is to say no. And if you have not eaten sweets for a week and you go to a wedding, you will not have dinner and just rush to the dessert counter. Starving yourself so much that you just binge when you see food you love is a very bad idea. The word 'no' only tempts a person further. You have to learn to have a good relationship with food and relish and enjoy it.

Whenever you eat any food, make sure it has many colours. Your food should be attractive and appealing. Red, green and orange food will make you want to eat it. Step one is to start being active. It is very easy to tell someone to climb the stairs and not take the lift. But even this is not easy for some people. And if you are late for a meeting, you are going to forget the stairs and hop into the lift. When you start exercising, you will realize on your own that you need to change your food habits. When you start working out, start recording your food intake for the first three days, even if it is as insignificant as a biscuit. You will realize how many mistakes you are making. And when you are ready to make that lifestyle change, it is an easy road from there.

Why yo-yo diets never help

Many people who need to lose weight try crash dieting, which is a short-term solution that will increase your body fat levels in the long term. Continual cycles of dieting, weight loss and weight gain are called yo-yo dieting. Yo-yo dieting does not help you to maintain a healthy body weight. Your body responds to these periods of semi-starvation by lowering its metabolic rate.

When you lose weight too quickly, you lose fat and muscle. Muscle burns calories, but fat does not. So, when you then stop dieting and eat normally again, your body will burn even fewer calories than before because the relative amount of muscle in your body has decreased and your metabolic rate is slower.

This is not the best way to take care of oneself. People who give up on diets after a week or a month have not fully understood why they need to make a change. Unless that mental shift happens, the best diet in the world will be of no help.

India-specific problems

80 per cent of your fitness is about the right diet. In India, everything we do is about food, whether it is a puja in the house or a family get-together. Food is the centre of our lives. We also have so many kinds of cuisines. With so many cultures come so many misunderstandings. Each culture has its own fads. In north India, everyone wants a paratha for breakfast. And that's fine as long as the portions are controlled. If you have a Marwari thali, your whole month's quota of calories is consumed in just one meal. That is why we need to make changes within the limitations of our cultures.

So many Indians suffer from deficiency of vitamin B12. And it is sad to see that doctors immediately recommend B12 injections to such people to make up for the deficit. I understand that they have to do that because the patient has reached that stage. But why didn't someone speak up before they reached that stage? So many people suffer from vitamin D3 deficiency because cosmetic surgeons tell them not to go out in the sun. But why? Because it causes skin damage. And then we apply sunscreen so many times a day that if we step out in the sun without it for even 10 minutes, the skin is damaged. A good thing like sunlight has been made bad by so-called cosmetic surgeons. Not going out in the sun can result in so many problems. It is so sad that in a country like India, where there is an abundance of sunlight, people suffer from vitamin D deficiencies.

THE MENACE OF SUPPLEMENTS

Too much of anything is always bad. Too much fat is bad, too much sugar is bad, and too much protein is bad. Anything that is in excess in your body is going to be stored as fat. Did you know that excess protein draws off all the calcium from your body? That results in an extra load on your kidneys. So you have to eat only what your body requires.

One of the most common supplements used by gym goers is whey protein. It is a high-quality protein powder made from cow's milk. Of the two proteins that milk has—casein and whey protein, the latter is more soluble and also has a higher quality rating. Creatine is a compound involved in the production of energy in the body. It is found in small amounts in red meat and fish. Creatine supplements are available in capsules or as a powder. Both whey supplements and creatine have side effects if taken in large quantities. Possible side effects of creatine include stomach cramps, nausea, diarrhoea, loss of appetite, muscle cramps and dehydration. High doses of creatine could potentially injure the kidneys, liver and heart.

I hear of so many cases of jaundice, which stems partly from excessive protein in the body. Jaundice is a warning sign that you should check what you are eating. There are so many people who live on protein shakes because their trainer tells them to. But they do not understand that the trainer does not know much about diet; his job is to only make sure you work out properly. Ask a dietician for advice. In my gyms, trainers are banned from discussing diets. Too much protein—especially lab-made protein—is very bad. That is why people have started bloating. Their systems cannot digest food properly. Their body is not able to release the enzymes and digestive juices that are needed because they are consuming lab-made food. Everyone should realize that this is a supplement. A supplement is something you take in addition to your everyday food. You need it if you are on a very special diet or are travelling and do not always have access to a balanced diet.

A lot of people ask me how I look so youthful even though I am 52 years old. I tell them it is because I rarely have protein shakes. I have tried them as well as aminos in the form of supplements. But I have not stuck to them because I like to eat as natural as possible. I do have protein bars if I am out and don't have a lot of time between meetings. Instead of having tea and biscuits, I have a more filling protein bar. That is when supplements are useful. Supplements are called so because they are meant to *supplement* your diet. They cannot become your main diet.

Follow this diet

While your diet will change according to your specific needs, what is mentioned below is a generic diet that anyone can follow.

TO LOSE WEIGHT:

Breakfast: Tea, 1 bowl of fresh fruit, a small bowl of oatmeal porridge

Mid-morning: 1 apple, coconut water

Lunch: Salad with sprouts, 2 rotis, green veggies, dal

Late afternoon: 1 cup of tea, 2 wheat crackers

Evening: Pomegranate and papaya

Dinner: Vegetable soup, platter of green veggies, low-fat paneer/tofu/chicken, 1–2 rotis

TO GAIN WEIGHT:

Early morning: Banana milkshake made with 2 bananas

Breakfast: Oatmeal porridge made with 4 tbsp of oatmeal

Lunch: 3 bajra/jowar rotis with ghee, 1 bowl of high-carb vegetables, 1 bowl of salad, 100 g paneer (made with skimmed or cow's milk)/soya paneer/chicken/fish and 2–4 eggs

Evening snack: Brown bread sandwich and 1 bowl of

sprouts with sweet potato (Snack options in between meals: fruits and dried fruits)

Pre-workout: 2 bananas or 1 large jacket potato

Post-workout: 1 banana with a whey-protein shake

Dinner: 3 chapatis/bajra rotis, 1 bowl of fresh vegetables, 1 bowl salad, 150 g paneer (made with skimmed or cow's milk)/soya paneer/chicken/fish

TO GAIN MUSCLE:

Early morning: 2 bananas with 1 glass of skimmed milk

Breakfast: 6 tbsp of oats/8 tbsp of muesli with omelette made of 3 egg whites and 1 yolk/soya bhurji

Lunch: 4–5 rotis with a little ghee/2 small bowls of brown rice with 1 bowl of mixed vegetables, 1 bowl of salad and 150 g paneer (made with skimmed or cow's milk)/soya paneer/chicken/fish

Snacks: 1 bowl of sprouts/egg-white sandwich (Snack options in between meals: fruits and dried fruits)

> Pre-workout: 2 bananas or 1 large jacket potato
>
> Post-workout: 1 banana with a whey-protein shake
>
> Dinner: 3 chapatis/bajra rotis, 1 bowl of fresh vegetables, 1 bowl salad, 150 g paneer (made with skimmed or cow's milk)/soya paneer/chicken/fish

GOOD FAD, BAD FAD

The rules are simple. There are things you can eat and others you must avoid. If you follow these points, you will always be healthy.

Things to avoid:
- Fried food
- Red meat
- Gravies—choose grilled instead
- Sweetened yoghurt
- Alcohol
- Cigarettes
- Large portions of desserts
- Yo-yo diets
- Skipping breakfast

- Eating a heavy dinner late at night

The good foods:
- Leafy, green vegetables
- Sprouts and salads
- Fruits—eat them raw, avoid juices
- Egg whites
- Tofu
- Olive oil
- Sesame and flax seeds
- Skimmed-milk products
- Multivitamin supplements if required
- Chilled yoghurt with fresh fruits

Never forget to exercise

What you eat is only one part of the weight-loss equation. Diet alone might help you drop the kilos, but you will have trouble keeping them off if you don't exercise. There is a big difference between weight loss via diet and weight loss via diet and exercise. The method that uses both is significantly healthier and leads to a body that is capable and strong. If you lose weight from diet alone, your health will suffer. Without exercise, you will be forced to maintain a very low-calorie diet, which is not particularly pleasant. Weight loss only through diet also puts the focus on the lack of food, instead of the growth and increase in strength and endurance that comes with exercise. Exercise increases your self-confidence, which ensures that you make smart food choices.

Chapter 7

Managing Your Lifestyle

STARTING A FITNESS PROGRAMME MAY be one of the best things you can do for yourself. After all, physical activity can reduce the risk of chronic disease, help you lose weight and even boost your self-esteem. And the benefits are yours for the taking, regardless of age, sex or physical ability.

Regular exercise can help you control your weight, reduce your risk of heart disease, and strengthen your bones and muscles. But if you have not exercised for some time and you have health concerns, talk to your doctor and your gym instructor before starting a new fitness routine. When you are designing your personal fitness programme, consider your fitness goals. Think about your likes and dislikes and then consider a practical way to keep your programme on track.

Life is stressful for everyone and there are challenges every day. And the best way you can deal with them is by facing the problems with a healthy mind and body. Starting a fitness programme is an important decision, but it does not have to be an overwhelming one. By planning carefully, pacing yourself and making small but significant changes, you can make fitness a healthy habit that lasts a lifetime.

Let me introduce you to a few people who have won the battle of the bulge. They decided to make themselves a priority and the results are for everyone to see.

Sagar Chopra, 34

'Before I realized I was in serious trouble, I had already started going to the gym. But I was not committed to it and for two years I was very irregular. When my two-year membership expired, I took a break for six months. During that time, I started eating a little too much—please keep my Punjabi genes in mind—and, before I knew it, my weight was 120 kg. My mother advised me to get my blood sugar level tested. It was absolutely in the red. I could not believe the number was 400—almost four times the normal level! I went to the doctor and I was given medication and told that I would have to take them for the rest of my life. I did not want to do that, so I asked him for options. The alternative suggested was a gastric bypass surgery, where your stomach is stapled so you consume much less food than you used to. But I asked him, "What if I wanted to lose weight on my own by dieting and exercising?" The doctor showed no faith in me and said that there was no way I would be able to manage because I am not committed. He even laughed at me for suggesting something like that.

'I, obviously, did not take it too well. In four-and-a-half months, I lost 40 kg. At my highest, my weight was 130 kg; I am now 105. I am still not at my ideal weight; I want to lose 25 kg more.

'Leena's lifestyle management programme taught me the importance of discipline. I have changed my eating habits. I learnt that we can do without the traditional roti–dal–chawal combo even though that is not a concept we Indians understand well. I now eat rotis maybe once or twice a week. I also don't eat very late in the night. There is nothing now that is a "major" meal for me. I have about 6–9 small meals every day. After I made that change, I realized I was much more energetic. I don't feel any lethargy now. There is also no over-the-top hunger. The most important change that has happened is that I sleep well at night now. Earlier, sleeping at night was a major problem. I was an insomniac. When I was overweight, my immunity levels were very low. I used to have a cough and cold almost every day. But that's not the case any more.

'As far as exercising went, I started out with very low weights with high repetition. When I was in my full glory, my stamina was very low. Just 7–10 minutes on the treadmill and I could feel death coming closer. But now, it's like the treadmill is tired of rolling, but I just can't stop. On the cross trainer, I could earlier manage to stay on just for 2–3 minutes. Now 30–40 minutes is a breeze for me. Also, my waist size used to be 51 inches. Now it is down to 36.

'There has been a lot of hard work and sincerity

Sagar Chopra

BEFORE   AFTER

behind the results. The constant encouragement always helps. Everyone remarks on how much better I look now. That is a huge boost. Leena would personally encourage me to push myself. I have seen her go to people talking on the phone while working out and telling them to do so at their personal time.

She did it because she is committed to seeing every one of her clients fit. Because of all this, gymming is kind of an addiction for me. Even if it is 1 a.m., I have my gym bag in the car so I don't miss out on my workout. I *have* to devote my 1–2 hours to the gym and I now work out six days a week.

'Any amount of money is useless if you do not enjoy good health. There is absolutely no substitute for good health. Today, because of me, my mother, my wife and seven or eight of my very good friends have joined the gym and work out regularly.'

Neha Malekar, 30

'Five years ago, I weighed 85 kg. That was after the delivery of my son. Within six months, it had come down to 72 kg. But after that the number just wouldn't change. That is when I knew that I had to start working out. My son was four months old when I started taking my fitness seriously. I used to go to the gym in the afternoon when it was usually empty and just three months later I lost around 13 kg! I had finally reached my ideal weight of 60 kg. Other than gymming, I used to climb all the twenty-seven

Neha Malekar

BEFORE   AFTER

storeys of my building twice a day. I would also jog for 45 minutes every day.

'When I had gained all that weight, I always stayed away from wearing the clothes I loved. I was just not confident about my looks. I had had enough of wearing frumpy clothes and wanted a change. Leena had put me on a lifestyle management programme and I was provided with a diet that I had to follow religiously. One day I used to work on my lower body and the next day would only be cardio. I also had to concentrate on my upper body because I had a lot of fat on my back.

'As for the diet, I used to have 1 bowl of oats for breakfast followed by juice around noon. After coming back from the gym in the afternoon, I would have 5–6 egg whites. That was followed by boiled chicken pieces and bhel at 4 p.m. I would end the day with soup at 7 p.m. I was completely off carbs. There was no rice or chapati for me, although I could have brown bread or brown rice or brown rotis with vegetables.

'My life has changed completely after I started concentrating on my fitness. I am so confident now. I can wear whatever I want and get so many compliments. Plus, I was featured in the *Mumbai Mirror* for my successful weight loss and Leena carried my pictures as part of her promotion material. This year, I participated in the Gladrags Mrs India contest and was one of the twenty-two finalists. I am also looking at modelling in advertisements. Ever since that day four years ago, I have never stopped going to the gym. If on rare days I do feel bored, I cycle, swim or dance.

'There was a time when there was no way I would have said the following sentence. But now that I am a new person, I can confidently say that if you look at me, there is no way you will think that I am the mother of a five-year-old.'

Chintu Talwar, 34

'I do consultancy for redevelopment of societies. That means I have to deal with so many society members. So if a society has twelve flats and each flat has four family members, I have to work with forty-eight people. That doesn't even include developers, builders and architects. So you can imagine how stressful my work life is. Thankfully, I found a place that takes care of all that stress—Leena's gym. Every evening, after a hard day's work, I work out and feel completely re-energized. Sometimes I feel like the load I carry on my shoulders throughout the day disappears in the gym. Working out has had a huge impact on my life. The fact that you look good is another benefit. I started going to the gym at twenty when my weight was just 50 kg. I wanted to put on some weight but ended up weighing 90 kg. Then, I wanted to get lean and have abs, so I brought down my weight to 70 kg. So I have had all types of bodies. Mentally too, working out has been great. I used to be very short-tempered. But I am a much calmer person now.'

Esra Janjua, 15

'There was a time I used to go through six boxes of pizza in a day. Studying can be stressful sometimes and I used to cope with it by eating. That meant that at only 14, my weight had ballooned to 86 kg. To bring it down, I started monitoring what I ate. I started concentrating on eating more protein and fewer carbs and avoided food that had empty calories. I also cut down on burgers and soft drinks. But I knew that getting healthy also meant working out. So I joined Leena's gym. Initially, I used to work out on my own, but managed to lose only half a kilo. It didn't help that I was not that serious about working out. So I decided to work with a personal

Esra Janjua

BEFORE

AFTER

trainer. And within four months, I lost 23 kg; my weight now hovers around 65 kg. The dietician at Leena's gym also helped me a lot with choosing the right foods to eat. Now, I am so glad I decided to opt for a personal trainer. It helped tremendously that there was someone to push me in the beginning.

Then later on I knew I could do it on my own. Before I lost weight, I couldn't get into nice clothes at all. I couldn't wear the dresses I wanted to at parties. Now I can do all of that. I don't mind being photographed now. I feel so good about myself and I can look at myself in the mirror without being embarrassed. I can run around without feeling tired and needing a break. I feel lighter and fitter. My focus has become better because of my active lifestyle and good food. It's a new me.'

CANDICE PINTO, MODEL

'I was quite a healthy girl and on the fuller side when I was growing up. But I didn't know if I was a big girl or a small girl because I didn't look at people like that. But I was pretty active in sports and that kept me healthy. I never planned to be a model; things just happened and here I am. And it has been a very long journey of hard work and determination to get to where I am right now. I never knew much about the importance of going to the gym. It was only after I entered the modelling industry that I became aware of it. I realized that just being thin and starving myself or skipping meals off and on only made me put on weight. It also made me lazy, and I used to be slow the whole day. That is when I knew that I would rather eat, look good and be healthy. Health has to be everyone's priority because if you don't have your health, how can you work and think?

'As I'm very passionate about my job, I believe I should respect what I do. I love working out because it makes me feel great. That way, I can also eat whatever I want, albeit in moderation. We only live once and I want to make the best of my life. Working out should be a necessity in our day-to-day lives because it keeps us charged to face the challenges of the day ahead.

'I have never been thin and I still don't consider myself to be a thin person. I have a very athletic body and I love it. I work towards maintaining it. No matter how tired I might be, that 30-minute run or 20 minutes of functional training makes me feel good. I never push myself to the limit, as my profession is quite demanding and I have to work round the clock at times. If I had to give someone fitness advice, I would say this: Don't follow what others are doing. Try working out every alternate day. If you get bored of exercising in the gym, go out for a jog or walk. Trying new techniques of working out makes it fun. Eat everything but in moderation. Be sure to get a good night's sleep and, lastly, work towards being happy.'

Digambar Bhalerao, 80

'I was seventy-two when I started going to her gym. My main aim was, and still is, to stay fit. And even if I say so myself, I am very fit. Since my purpose is not to develop muscles, I use light dumb-bells and do cardio. In your old age, your mind isn't always stable. So people my age go to meditation classes or to a temple in order to get peace of mind. But they don't realize that if you want peace of mind, you must have a fit and healthy body. Just concentrating on mental well-being without looking after your physical well-being is not going to help you. Only a sound body can have a strong mind.'

POINTS TO PONDER

- Life is stressful for everyone and there are challenges every day. And the best way to deal with them is to face them with a healthy mind and body.

- Regular exercise can help you control your weight, reduce the risk of heart disease, and strengthen your bones and muscles.

- By planning carefully, pacing yourself and making small but significant changes, you can make fitness a healthy habit that lasts a lifetime.

Chapter 8

Popular Problems

I GET A LOT OF queries from people who frequent my gym about the changes they need to make in their diet for a fit and healthy body. While the following Q&As apply to the specific people who have asked me their questions, these diets are mostly generic and can help most people.

I am a 30-year-old housewife. My height is 5'2" and I weigh 72 kg. I joined a gym a month ago and am a vegetarian. What diet will help me lose weight?

You need to lose about 18–20 kg, as you are overweight. Exercise and diet will help you lose weight.

Early morning (7 a.m.): 1 fruit + 1 glass of skimmed milk

Breakfast (10 a.m.): 4 tbsp oats (or wheat flakes)/6 tbsp muesli in skimmed milk/1 bowl dalia/1 bowl upma or poha

Lunch (1 p.m.): 2 dry rotis + 1 bowl green vegetables + 1 bowl salad + 1 bowl dal + 1 bowl skimmed curd + 100 g skimmed paneer/soya paneer

Pre-workout (3 p.m.): 1 slice of wheat bread/egg sandwich + 1 glass of skimmed milk as coffee or tea

Post-workout (5 p.m.): 1 khakra/2 digestive biscuits/dry bhel + 1 bowl curd/1 glass buttermilk

Dinner (8.30 p.m.): 1 dry roti + 1 bowl green vegetables + 1 bowl salad + 1 bowl dal + 100 g skimmed paneer/soya paneer

I am 22, my height is 157 cm and my weight is 38 kg. Can you suggest a vegetarian diet for me to gain weight and plan my pregnancy?

You are too underweight and need to put on 8–10 kg.

With this weight, if you are planning a pregnancy, there is a chance of the baby being underweight. Try to put on weight with healthy foods.

Early morning (7 a.m.): 1 fruit + 1 glass of skimmed milk

Breakfast (9 a.m.): 1 bowl upma or poha/2 slices of brown-bread sandwich with paneer

Mid-morning (12 p.m.): 1 fruit + fistful of peanuts/ 4 pieces of almonds + 2 pieces of walnuts

Lunch (2.30 p.m.): 4–5 dry rotis + 1 bowl green vegetables + 1 bowl salad + 1 bowl skimmed curd/1 glass buttermilk + 100 g skimmed paneer chunks

Snack (5 p.m.): 2 slices of khakra/4 wheat toasts + 1 glass skimmed milk

Mid-evening (7 p.m.): Sprouts/brown-bread sandwich with vegetable

Dinner (9.30 p.m.): 4–5 dry rotis + 1 bowl green vegetables + 1 bowl salad + 1 bowl skimmed curd + 100 g skimmed paneer chunks

I am a 20-year-old girl weighing 52 kg and my height

is 5'6". I have fat on my tummy, waistline and thighs. Please suggest a diet and exercises to help me get rid of the fat.

According to your height, your ideal weight should be 60–62 kg. So you are not overweight, but you just need to take care of the quality of foods you eat so that you can reduce fat and gain muscle mass. Incorporate these simple instructions into your diet.

- Do not skip meals, especially your breakfast. Instead of eating 2 heavy meals, opt for 4–5 small and frequent meals.
- Always use skimmed milk (i.e., milk without cream) for tea, coffee, curd and paneer.
- Eat at least 2 fruits every day.
- Increase protein intake in the form of skimmed milk, curd, paneer, dal, pulses, sprouts, tofu, soy milk, soy chunks, de-skinned chicken, lean fish, egg whites, etc.
- Make sure you exercise regularly.
- Drink at least 2–3 litres of water every day.
- Avoid sweets, chocolates, ice creams, soft drinks, cakes, etc.

- Avoid eating junk food.
- Avoid organ meats, mutton, egg yolk and fried fish.
- Avoid refined food such as maida.
- Join a gym and start your workout as prescribed for your age by your trainers; you need to live an active life.

I have been eating out a lot recently and now I want to go on a detox diet. How should I go about it?

Everyone should go on detox on a regular basis to cleanse the body of toxins. Here is how you should start:

Early morning: 1 tall glass of lukewarm water followed by a 30-minute brisk walk and then stretching.

Breakfast: Oats, wheat crackers

Snack between meals: 1 cup of green tea or coconut water or fruits like papaya and orange

Lunch: 2 wholewheat rotis without ghee or oil, 1 bowl of sprouted moong and raita

Snack between meals: Regular tea followed by 1 cup of green tea or coconut water or fruits

Dinner: Brown-rice pulao, raita

Follow this for two days. On the second day, you could include paneer in the diet.

I am 24 years old and my height is 5'7". I want to increase my height.

You are already tall enough for an average Indian woman. Also, you cannot increase your height now, as it depends on the growth of your bones, which stops at the age of 18. But you can still improve your posture through yoga or by joining the gym.

I am 18 years old, my height is 5'5" and I weigh 65 kg. I have gained weight around my neck and face. Please suggest a vegetarian food plan and exercise to lose weight.

According to your height and age, your weight should be around 56–60 kg. This is the diet you should follow:

Early morning: 1 glass of lukewarm water + 2–3 soaked almonds + 1 walnut

Breakfast: 1 glass of skimmed milk + 2 tsp of Protinex + dalia porridge/1 cup of boiled moong sprouts

Mid-morning: 1 glass of buttermilk

Lunch: 1 bowl of salad, 2 chapatis without oil or ghee + ½ bowl of rice, 1½ bowls of dal or sambar or skimmed-milk paneer + 1 cup of vegetables, 1 cup of skimmed-milk curd

Evening snack: 1 wholewheat sandwich (avoid butter) or 2 idlis with sambar or 1 plain dosa

Mid-evening: 1 seasonal fruit

Dinner: Like lunch, but avoid rice

Exercise: Start playing an outdoor sport and then join a gym.

I am 19, weigh 60 kg and am 5'3". Can you suggest a diet plan?

You need to lose 5 kg. You can follow this diet:

Early morning: 1 glass of lukewarm water + juice of ½ a lemon

Breakfast: Soya milk + 2–3 egg whites + 1 roti or 1 plate of seviya upma with vegetables

Mid-morning: 1 fruit

Lunch: 1 bowl of salad + 2 rotis + 1 bowl of rice + 1½ cups of dal or dahi kadhi + 1 cup of vegetables + 1 cup of skimmed-milk curd

Evening snack: 1 cup of tea with ½ tsp sugar + chana chat/2–3 steamed dhoklas

Dinner: 1 bowl of vegetable soup + 1 jowar/bajra/ragi roti + 2 pieces of chicken or grilled fish + 1 cup of vegetables

I am 26 years old, 5'1" in height and weigh about 54 kg. I want to reduce my weight to 50 kg. I suffer from thyroid and use Thyronorm 50 mcg daily. Also, my breast size is 36 and I wanted to reduce that too. I do not eat fast food or stuff that is fried. Do advise a diet plan.

The breast is one of the areas where a woman is prone

to put on fat, but it can be reduced with diet and exercise, so it is better to join a gym and workout.

Early morning: 1 fruit + 1 glass of skimmed-milk

Breakfast: 4 tbsp oats/wheat flakes/6 tbsp muesli in skimmed milk/1 bowl of dalia, upma or poha

Lunch: 2 dry roti + 1 bowl of green vegetables + 1 bowl of salad + 1 bowl of dal + skimmed curd + 100 g skimmed paneer/soya paneer

Snack: 1 khakara/2 digestive biscuits/dry bhel + curd/buttermilk/tea

Dinner: 1 dry roti + 1 bowl of green vegetables + 1 bowl of salad + 1 bowl of dal + skimmed curd + 100 g skimmed paneer/soya paneer

Consume 3–4 litres of water a day and do not use more than 2 tsp oil per day.

Continue with your medicines.

I'm an 18-year-old girl, my height is 5'4" and I weigh 63 kg. Most of my weight is concentrated around the lower part of my body and thighs. Please suggest a diet plan.

According to your height, your weight should be around 55 kg. You can follow this diet.

Morning: 1 glass of warm water + juice of ½ a lemon (no sugar/salt/honey)

Breakfast: 1 glass of skimmed milk + 2–3 idlis/1 dosa with green chutney or sambhar (avoid coconut or groundnut chutney)/muesli with skimmed milk/2–3 egg-white omelettes with wholewheat bread

Mid-morning: 1 seasonal fruit (avoid banana/chikoo/custard apple/mango)

Lunch: Start with 1 glass of water + 1 bowl of salad + 2 dry rotis + 1 cup rice + 1 bowl of dal/sprouts + 1 bowl of vegetables + 1 cup of curd/1 glass of thin buttermilk

Evening snack: 1 cup of green tea + 2–3 multigrain biscuits/1 wholewheat sandwich (no butter)/dry bhel (no sev/puri)

7 p.m.: 1 seasonal fruit

Dinner: 1 bowl of mixed vegetable soup + 1 bowl of salad + 2 dry rotis (avoid rice) + 1½ bowls of dal/2–3 pieces of chicken/steamed grilled fish + 1 cup of vegetables

I am a 21-year-old girl, my weight is 51 kg and my height is 5'7". Please suggest a vegetarian diet that would help me gain weight.

Early morning: A handful of soaked almonds + dates + raisins + cashews + pistachios

Breakfast: 1 glass of skimmed milk + 2 tsp of protein powder + 2 parathas stuffed with paneer or vegetables/1 bowl of cornflakes/wheat flakes with skimmed milk and sugar with fruits/1 bowl of sprouts

Mid-morning: 1–2 seasonal fruits/fruit juice

Lunch: 3 rotis + 2 bowls of rice + 1½ cups of dal/soya chunks + 1 bowl of vegetables + 1 bowl of salad + 1 bowl of curd

Evening: 1 glass of fruit milkshake/soya milk + 4–5 steamed dhokla/corn chat/nachani sheera

Mid-evening: 1 fruit

Dinner: 2 bhakris + 1–2 cups of rice/khichdi + 1½ cups of dal/paneer bhurji + 1 bowl of vegetables + 1 bowl of salad

Bed time: Fruit custard

I am 15 and I weigh 30 kg. I am 4'9". Please help me with a diet plan that will help me gain weight and grow taller. I'm vegetarian.

Considering you are just 15, you have almost three to four years to grow. You shouldn't be worried. The average Indian height is around 5'3" to 5'6", and the average weight is 50–55 kg. The increase in height also depends on your genetics and the release of certain hormones. Let nature take its course. You can only help yourself by cycling or swimming regularly. These activities boost your appetite. However, avoid fried and junk food.

I am 37, weigh 63 kg and am 5'4". I want to lose some fat around my stomach, hips and waist. My biggest problem is my work life, which leaves me exhausted and with no time to exercise. I have also stopped eating lunch. Please suggest a vegetarian diet plan that will help me stay fit despite my lifestyle.

You are making several very common mistakes. Never go on a foodless diet. Have a decent breakfast. Follow it up with a snack or some soup an hour before lunch. Have lunch, and then eat some fruit in the evening. The smallest meal of the day should be your dinner (a milkshake or only soup). You are getting exhausted because you are skipping lunch. Start going for morning or evening walks to get some exercise. Try this for a month and you should be happy with the results.

WHAT I DO

And finally, here's what I eat and how I work out:

Day 1: I start my week with power yoga and spinning.

Day 2: The second day starts with functional training, a weight training routine targeted at the core, abdomen and back muscles. I start with 3 rounds of bench presses, followed by 20 reps of pulley rowing with jump squats. I then work on the Russian swing, a kind of kettlebell workout. The routine tops off with the unilateral chest press, off bench rear delt in squat position and lateral raises with squats. I practise Ashtanga yoga in the evenings.

Day 3: The third day's workout is the same as day one—power yoga and spinning.

Day 4: On day four, I start with 3 sets of jump squats (20 reps each) and go on to do the same with leg curls, full squats, leg extensions and bridging. I then do 2 sets of split lunges, 50 reps in each set and practise Ashtanga yoga in the evening.

Day 5: Once again, like the first day of the week, day five also begins with power yoga and spinning. I include Flowin Friction core strengthening to my routine, which gives the body a full workout. It focuses on strengthening all body muscles.

Day 6: I end the week's workout with body weight training followed by push-ups and jumping jacks, jump squats and planks, body weight rowing and burpees, (a combination of a jump squat and a plank), high jumps and step-ups.

Day 7: Rest

My workout strikes a balance in everything—muscle building, strengthening, cardio for stamina and yoga for de-stressing. I follow a diet that aids my strenuous workout routine and is focused on building muscles and strengthening them. I also start the day with one litre of warm water. This helps flush out all the toxins. I also cross-train a lot, which includes weight training.

This is what my daily diet includes:

Early morning: Neem juice or coconut water

Pre-workout: A banana or an apple

Breakfast: Regular home-cooked food

Mid-morning: Fruit or almonds or 1 cup of green tea

Lunch: 1 bhakri, lots of veggies, 1 bowl curd, 1 glass buttermilk

Afternoon: Black coffee with 1 digestive biscuit

Evening: Soya cutlet or tofu sandwich

Dinner: Bhakri with vegetables and soup

PRE- AND POST-WORKOUT MEALS

Pre- and post-workout meals are the meals you eat before and after working out. Once you ensure you are eating right throughout the day, the meals directly surrounding your workouts are next in line in terms of the amount of impact they have on the results you get. What you eat before your workout is crucial for fuelling the workout itself and maximizing your performance overall. What you eat after your workout is crucial for optimizing the recovery process, which begins as soon as your workout ends, and ensuring that your body has all of the supplies it needs in order to recover. When you eat carbohydrate-rich foods before exercise, you will perform better mentally and physically during your workout.

Eat these before your workout

Oatmeal

Having oatmeal is great, especially before your morning workouts when you are running on an empty stomach and you cannot have a meal a couple of hours before your workout. Oatmeal is known to settle well and it's also a great source of energy. If you can add some fruit to your oatmeal, there's nothing like it.

Protein shakes

These are very popular among those who hit the gym. Protein is extremely important for overall development of the muscles, bones and even skin. A protein shake is good if you do not receive an adequate amount from natural sources. For athletes and people doing regular workouts, it is fine to have a protein shake after a workout, but not every couple of hours. But egg whites and yolk are a better alternative to protein shakes. If you are a vegetarian, soya and tofu are a good choice.

Yoghurt

It contains calcium and proteins and some natural sugar. Because it is easy on the stomach and the digestive system, it is a great option. Add some fruits or honey to yoghurt for a quick energy boost.

Smoothies

Fruit smoothies are rich in complex carbohydrates and the yoghurt delivers the protein punch. They are recommended both before and after the workout as they are easily digested. The carbohydrate in the fruit breaks down quickly and the protein helps prevent muscle damage.

Eat these after your workout

Eggs

Protein and carbs are the two keys to a good post-workout meal. Eggs have the former covered. At just 70 calories each, eggs pack 6.3 g of protein and are one of the few foods that naturally contain vitamin D. Also, raw eggs are no better than overcooked ones. In fact, eating cooked eggs allows your body to absorb almost twice the amount of protein.

Soya and tofu

250 g should be had for an adequate amount of post-workout protein.

Bananas

They are high in the good carbs you need after a workout. Their fast-acting carbs will help restore your body's levels of glycogen, which helps rebuild damaged muscles. And they provide lots of potassium.

Dried fruit and nuts

If you do not have time to sit and have a meal after your workout, a handful of dried fruit and nuts delivers a quick protein and carbs fix. Soy nuts are especially helpful for building muscle.

Pineapples

They contain bromelain, a natural anti-inflammatory that has been proven to heal bruises, sprains and swelling. They are also high in vitamin C, a key component in repairing tissue.

Your body uses a lot of energy during a workout. If you do not replenish it within 1–2 hours after finishing, your muscles will break down to give energy, and all your hard work could go to waste. Even a little food within 15 minutes of working out goes a long way. So this meal is crucial.

POSTURE

There is a close link between good posture and how people feel about themselves in general. Posture

is important in everything you do. Bad posture can lead to back pain, and even make you feel more tired than usual. Good posture will influence many things in your life, such as your risk of experiencing lower back pain, your energy levels, as well as your focus and concentration. If you are constantly in a slouched position all day long, this is going to mean that there is far less oxygen coming into the body, and low levels of oxygen are one of the contributing factors to fatigue development. That is why proper posture is a must to help boost energy levels. Good posture promotes good health by keeping your bones and joints aligned so muscles are properly used. It decreases wear and tear on joints, decreases ligament stress, keeps the spine strong, prevents fatigue, strain and overuse, and promotes an overall confident appearance.

Imagine you have a silver thread that runs through

your body, linking your bones and muscles in proper alignment. This is what good posture looks like when the silver thread is in control:

- When standing, your body is vertically aligned, with a straight spine and head, and a straight line from your ankles to your knees, hips, shoulders and ears.
- Your shoulders and hips are levelled, and knees face straight ahead when you walk or stand.
- The arms hang loosely, with the palms facing the side of the body.
- There is a slight inward curve to your lower back when standing.
- Your abdomen is flat, pulled in and up.
- When you sit, you sit up straight, with your head up and don't lean forward.

Forward head

The forward head posture is one of the most common postural problems in our lifestyle. It happens when you bend your head while typing or reading, drive with your head more than 2–3 inches away from the headrest, carry a backpack or heavy purse slung

over one shoulder. So make sure the top of your computer screen is level with your eyes. Carry the backpack over both shoulders to balance the weight distribution. And if you carry a heavy purse, it is better to sling it diagonally across your body.

Fix it: Lie face down on the floor, with your hands overlapped and held on your lower back. Lift and extend only your head and shoulders up, while squeezing your shoulder blades together. Hold for 3 seconds, and repeat fifteen times. Do this thrice a day.

Kyphosis

Here, your upper back looks as if it is rounding out a bit. While it is not painful, it can play a major role in neck, shoulder and upper back pain. Without proper attention, a humpback can become a major issue. By having the head further forward than is natural for the spine, the body will compensate for the extra weight by overworking the muscles which support the neck and head. This means that muscles that are normally used are being placed under excess strain.

Fix it: Stand in a corner facing the wall with your arms bent at the elbow at shoulder level. With your hands against the opposite wall, lean into the corner. Repeat this five times.

Rounded shoulders

Rounded shoulders are usually the result of slouching. Prolonged slouching can strain the muscles between the shoulder blades, causing pain in the upper back. Here, your shoulders sag. As a result, you have a sunken chest and

protruding shoulder blades. Round shoulders also compress your diaphragm, which leads to shallow breathing. Proper posture allows proper breathing and sufficient oxygen intake.

Fix it: Squeeze your shoulder blades down and together, and bring both arms and hands behind you. Grab the right elbow with the left hand. Take a few deep breaths. Lift your chest and keep your shoulder blades down and back. Now repeat by grabbing your left elbow with your right hand.

Scoliosis

Have you noticed that one hip seems to move easier than the other or that you usually carry your parcels or kids on one side or the other? Scoliosis causes 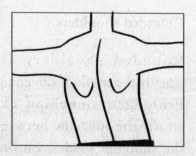 one hip to be pushed forward or one shoulder to sit higher than the other. It is a sideways curve of the spine that causes stiffness and pain. Improving and maintaining your posture is essential for living with scoliosis.

Fix it: Stand with your feet about 18 inches apart and extend your arms parallel to the ground. With bent knees, move your hips forward, then bring them back to the neutral position, then move them backwards, then to the right, then to the left.

Lordosis

Here, your lower back is a little arched. With an extreme curve, the lower spine will have a deep curve, causing the abdomen to stick out and causing the hip areas to curve back and up. 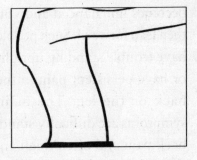 This can happen because of bad posture, family genetics, injury or illnesses of the spine. This often comes from being overweight. When a person carries too much weight in the stomach area, it pulls the back forward.

Fix it: Stand with your back to the wall and your heels an inch away from the wall. Lift one knee as high as you can, grasping it in your hands and pulling it to your body. Count till 10. Repeat using the other leg. Repeat four times with each leg.

Flat back

Here, the spine loses its natural lower back curve and becomes flat. The spine becomes imbalanced and you then lean forward. Such people have trouble standing upright or have persistent pain in the back or the leg. The main  symptoms are difficulty standing upright with lower back pain and often thigh and groin pain.

Fix it: Hip isolations are a good exercise for this problem. Focus on extending the position that moves towards the back. Exercises to strengthen your core, buttocks, neck and rear shoulder muscles and back extensions are recommended to help correct a flat back.

Sunken chest

Here, your chest is noticeably sunken. This can reduce your breathing space and can also influence how you feel about yourself. Chest up and shoulders back, you tend to feel more confident, more in charge.

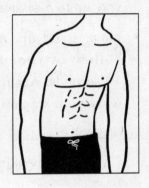

Fix it: Place the back of the right hand on the right side of your face, pressing the elbow straight back. Keeping the elbow back, reach backward with the right hand. Repeat four times. Then repeat on the left side, holding the right arm in position.

When you are at work

Here are a couple of quick stretches that are office-friendly:

- On your office chair, sit with your knees spread apart. Bend forward to the floor until you feel a comfortable stretch in your back. Hold for 10 seconds. Try doing 3 sets of this, working your way up to 5 sessions per day.

- Now, stand up. Arch your back to make the hollow of your back deeper. Hold this for 10 seconds. Again, try doing 3 sets of this, and work your way up to 5 sessions per day.

> ### POINTS TO PONDER
>
> - The word 'no' only tempts a person further. You have to learn to have a good relationship with food and relish and enjoy it.
>
> - A good thing like sunlight has been made bad by so-called cosmetic surgeons. Not going out in the sun can result in so many problems. It is so sad that in a country like India, where there is an abundance of sunlight, people suffer from vitamin D deficiencies.

- A supplement is something you take in addition to your everyday food. You need it if you are on a very special diet or are travelling and do not always have access to a balanced diet.

Conclusion

The Leena Mogre Way

ONE OF THE DEFINING MOMENTS in my career was starting my academy. The word 'fitness' didn't even exist then, so a fitness academy was a long shot. A lot of my friends even said that it wouldn't be a good idea. But that was my first move towards this career. The aerobics and personal training I used to do was for fun. I had done my master's in nutrition and I was thinking about setting up a diet clinic. But I never got around to it. But this academy showed me the potential of the fitness industry. Even though I was the only one to have such an academy, which turned out to be a pioneer of fitness education, there were so many trainers who wanted to get certified.

So many people wanted to change their careers and become trainers.

Opening my first gym was also a milestone. After spending four years helping an international chain of gyms set up branches in India, I moved on to start my own gym. It was actually meant to start off as an academy. But within seven months, I had over 1000 members. I was so overwhelmed by the response that I had to shift to a bigger place. That was another milestone. In the course of time, I have realized that I need good lawyers and chartered accountants and advisors to run a business. You need a lot more than passion to succeed. But you have to be passionate about the field you are working in. That is what has sustained me even in the lowest moments of my career.

The first two things that come to mind when one thinks of a healthy lifestyle are diet and exercise. But why is a healthy lifestyle important? Better lifestyle habits will reduce the risk of heart attack; you will feel better, have more energy and reduce the risk of illness. A study conducted by Northwestern University confirmed that a healthy lifestyle has the biggest impact on cardiovascular health. The majority of people who adopted healthy lifestyle habits in young adulthood maintained a low cardiovascular risk profile in middle age. The five most important healthy behaviours, the study found, are low or no alcohol intake, not smoking, weight control, physical activity and a healthy diet. Living healthy also elevates your mood, helping you feel happy and have more self-confidence, which results in a better quality of life. But being healthy is a lifestyle choice and something that has to be achieved over time, not overnight.

That is why I reiterate again and again that you need to make fitness your lifestyle. It has to be inculcated as part of your routine and life. Fitness is not just exercise; it is also about diet, recuperation, sleep, understanding your body and instilling a healthy lifestyle. Fitness is a very simple concept; most people just complicate it because they are too lazy to work out. After reading this book, even if I manage to get a few people to change their habits and lives, it will be a success.

A Note on the Author

LEENA MOGRE IS INDIA'S FIRST woman personal fitness trainer, Madhuri Dixit being her first client followed by John Abraham, Bipasha Basu, Sameera Reddy, Katrina Kaif and Isha Koppikar, among others. Leena was the first Indian CEO of an international gym chain and was responsible for setting up and expanding this chain in India. She runs her own signature brand of fitness centres—Leena Mogre's Fitness—in Bandra, Shivaji Park and Thane in Mumbai, and Chandigarh. She was also associated with shows like *Nach Baliye* and *Bigg Boss*. Leena Mogre's Fitness is also the official trainer for Gladrags (Megamodels, Manhunt and Mrs India) and Elite Models.

Leena has a master's in food science and nutrition, specializing in sports medicine and injuries. She taught food science and nutrition at SNDT University, Mumbai, for a year. She is a pioneer of fitness education, and has trained more than 18,000 students till date. She has won the Indian Merchant Chamber (Women's Chapter) Business Woman of the Year award, the Mumbai Mayor's Award, 2008, and WAVES Woman of the Year—Fitness award. She is currently pursuing her PhD in nutrition. She lives in Mumbai with her family. This is her debut book.

A Note on the Author

THE ACADEMY

LM—The Fitness Academy was started in 1994. It has trained 18,000 personal trainers, and offers courses on fitness management, power yoga and kick-boxing.

Acknowledgements

I WAS NOT AN OVERNIGHT success. It has been a long journey and whatever I am today and everything that I have achieved is thanks to a lot of people. The people who have been with me are my brand. This book has given me the opportunity to thank them.

I begin by thanking my mother, Mrs Sanjeevani Pendse, for encouraging me to join SVT College of Home Science and to enroll in a gym when I was in college.

My mother-in-law, Mrs Nalini Mogre, was very supportive of my timings and also encouraged me to complete my master's degree after marriage.

My husband, Nikhil, has been my backbone, and also joined my business. My son, Arjun, of course, is very proud of me.

I thank my father-in-law, Mr Keshav Mogre,

Acknowledgements

who took care of my son when he was as young as 9 months, and encouraged me to take up fitness as my career. He was a bodybuilding enthusiast himself. I still remember that he used to preserve my press cuttings and show it to all and wear my branded T-shirts with pride everywhere, sometimes even at functions.

Thank you, Malini Patel, for helping me whenever I needed help.

Gauri Naiknavre and Hemant Naiknavre stood by me when I started my academy in Pune.

I can't forget Sameer Randive for his expert 'computer analysis'.

Mr Nitin Sardesai and Yash Sardesai for being there whenever I needed them.

Special thanks to Dr Ajit Vaze, Dr Nitin Dange and all my other doctor friends for being there for my husband when he was in the hospital.

Shyam Sanghvi and Dr Avinash Phadke—one call and they were there, no questions asked.

My friends—Vibha, Ajay Bharti, Ulhas Seema, Rahul Limaye and Aditi, among others.

Bobby and Priya Garg—Leena Mogre's Fitness's Chandigarh franchisees.

Acknowledgements

Heartfelt gratitude to my loyal staff for staying with me through all the ups and downs of the company. That is what has made us strong.

Above all, thanks to my loyal members all over Mumbai and India, and the students of my academy, without whom there is no me.

A Note on the Type

SABON IS AN OLD-STYLE serif typeface designed by the German-born typographer and designer Jan Tschichold (1902–1974) in the period 1964–1967. It was released jointly by the Linotype, Monotype, and Stempel type foundries in 1967. The design of the roman is based on types by Claude Garamond (c.1480–1561), particularly a specimen printed by the Frankfurt printer Konrad Berner. Berner had married the widow of a fellow printer Jacques Sabon, the source of the face's name, who had bought some of Garamond's type after his death. The italics are based on types designed by a contemporary of Garamond's, Robert Granjon. The typeface is frequently described as a Garamond revival.